Janice,

It has been good working with you.

God bless you

Jeanne Chazzell

GOD'S GIFT

JEANNE HOBSON CHAPPELL

THE ALABASTER BOX
P. O. Box 819
Oologah, OK 74053-0819

- *Italicized names are fictitious*

II

GOD'S GIFT

TABLE OF CONTENTS:

ACKNOWLEDGMENTS

This book is dedicated to Jesus Christ – the One who inspired it. Without God's faithful pursuit of my soul, this story would never have been written.

I especially want to thank all who were used of God to show me His will, His power and His glory – those who set my feet on His path.

I want to thank everyone who helped and encouraged me along the way. With a special thanks to Jeanie, Helen and Charles, for their support and with God's guidance, edited my manuscript.

I want to thank my family who supported me every step of the way: my husband Mike, daughter Shawna, son Michael, daughter-in-law Jen, and grandchildren, Sefanie, Zoe, Destiny and Justin. I love you all.

CHAPTER ONE

GOD, WHAT WILL YOU SHOW ME?

The 10th of June, 1996, had been a long day, and I was exhausted. I had not slept well the last few days so my husband, Mike, shut off the TV before 10:00. Neither of us felt we could watch a rerun of the 6:00 news, so we went to bed. I had drifted off to sleep when the phone rang.

My brother, Dicky, who was four years older than I, was a K-9 Officer for the Tulsa Police Department, and an eighteen-year veteran. At midnight we got a call that Dicky had been shot and was in surgery, but they were not sure how serious it was.

At the hospital, we found that Dicky was shot in the right side with a twenty-gauge shotgun. The doctor removed part of his liver and one kidney. Dicky died twice in surgery, and once the defibrillator couldn't revive him, so the doctor performed hand heart massage to bring him back. At one

1

point the nurse said Dicky's blood pressure was good, and after the doctor closed him up we could see him. Every minute seemed like an hour, but it sounded hopeful that Dicky would survive.

A short time later, because Dicky was unstable, we were moved to a private waiting room. Only then were we told how serious he was. Dicky's blood volume was replaced seven times, which depleted the hospital's blood supply, and he still lost fluid. The nurse said we could go in pairs to see him, because his chance of survival was not good. Shortly after the first two returned, the nurse said they were doing CPR on him and checking for brain waves.

I prayed that God would leave Dicky for a while longer. I prayed that if he was not saved prior to the gunfight, or in the ambulance, if God chose to take him that God forgive Dicky's sins and receive his soul into heaven.

"If we confess our sins, he is faithful and just to forgive us our sins, and to cleanse us from all unrighteousness." (I John 1:9) *"For by grace are ye saved through faith; and that not of yourselves: it is the gift of God:"* (Eph 2:8)

"God's Gift" / J. H. Chappell

I know you cannot pray the sinner's prayer for someone. They have to confess their sins and receive Jesus by faith. But I prayed it anyway. God took Dicky a few minutes later at four forty-eight, the morning of June 11, 1996.

When we went in to see Dicky, he looked huge to me. I would not understand why until three years later when my co-worker, Lisa, and her two sons were saved. The night they received Jesus as their Savior, I was taken aback because all three of them looked larger than normal. Then I understood when the glory of God is on someone, their size is magnified. The Glory of God was on Dicky.

In spite of Dicky's massive size, he had a peaceful look on his face. When I heard the nurse say he was gone, my biggest fear became reality. *This is it! This is what it feels like to lose someone you love.* God had me in the palm of His hand, because I felt like I was wrapped in a warm blanket.

"God is our refuge and strength, a very present help in trouble." (Psalm 46:1) *"Peace I leave with you, my peace I give unto you: not as the world giveth, give I unto you. Let not your heart be troubled, neither let it be afraid."* (John 14:27)

"God's Gift" / J. H. Chappell

On the ride home I thought, *God, what are you going to show me through this? Jesus, I feel Your arms around me, but I wish I knew that Dicky was saved ...*

Mom and **Dad** in front. In birth order from the oldest to the youngest: **Norman, Ronny** holding his granddaughter, **Dicky, Danny, Jeanne,** and **Daryl (Chub).** July 4, 1995

4

Front row: **Jeanne** before her 8th birthday, **Dicky** age 12, **Danny** age 10, and **Daryl (Chub)** age 6
Back row: **Ronny** age 14, **Mom, Dad** and **Norman** before his 16th birthday. April, 1963

"God's Gift" / J. H. Chappell

On February 29, 1996, God put it on my heart to write my brothers and explain salvation. With four older brothers and one younger God knew I could not witness to them face to face and explain all He wanted them to know. If God wanted to reach my brothers, I would set my fears aside and do what He asked. Still, it was one of the hardest letters I had ever written. I wrote in part:

"I don't know if you realized, when I had my hysterectomy in 1994, it abscessed and could have killed me. My life turned in a new direction. So, before anything serious happens to you or to me, I need to straighten out a few things we were taught growing up.

"I used to wonder why I was born, because I could not believe the way the church taught and could never be good enough to go to heaven. You don't have to work at salvation – it is a free gift! *[For by grace are ye saved through faith; and that not of yourselves: it is the gift of God: Not of works, lest any man should boast."]* (Eph 2:8-9)

"This subject is hard to talk about, so God put it on my heart to write you.

"When I went to a Baptist church in 1978, I was afraid to go forward because I didn't know what to do, or what to expect. I hated to be in front of people and feared embarrassment. If I had told the pastor that I wanted to surrender my life to Jesus, he would have quietly led me in prayer. Then we would have announced that I accepted Jesus as my Savior. Easy, huh? But no one explained it to me. Afraid, I left the church lost. I called a deacon when I got home, and he and the pastor met me back at the church where I was saved in private. I was later baptized in Oologah Lake. After it was over, I didn't know why it scared me.

"I know you believe Jesus is the Son of God, and He died to save us from our sins. Ask Jesus to forgive you, a sinner, of your sins and come into your heart. At that moment you are **saved!** Tell at least one person as a testimony of your profession of faith. I would love for you to tell me.

"A pastor doesn't have to be present, you can be saved while driving your car or in your home; you can be saved anywhere. Salvation is **free.** All you have to do is **ask.**

"When God forgives your sins, they are forgiven forever. *["As far as the east is from the west, so far hath he removed our transgressions from us."]* (Psalm 103:12)

"Now comes the hard part; you have to forgive yourself and forget your past sins. Don't drag them around so you doubt your salvation. **You are saved!** When you sin, ask God to forgive you and strive to do better. Don't let anyone make you doubt your salvation, because in Ephesians 1:13, it says we are sealed with the Holy Spirit.

"God's Gift" / J. H. Chappell

"When you find a church you like, tell the pastor you are saved and wish to be baptized. If you don't want to be baptized in front of the whole congregation, ask if you can be baptized with only your family and few close friends present.

"You don't have to be a Bible scholar before you attend Sunday School or church. Everyone starts at the beginning. What matters is that you learn about Jesus and build a relationship with Him.

"I love you too much not to share this.

"Love,

Jeanne."

Thankful I wrote the letter three and half months earlier, I thought about the way we were raised and how opposed to the church we became. Only by the grace of God had He touched any of our hearts.

CHAPTER TWO

GOD, PLEASE HEAR MY CRY

When I was four years old, we started to attend fundamental, non-denominational meetings that Mom was raised in. Services were held in homes instead of churches. Sometimes they got access to larger buildings for special meetings, where workers (preachers) came to preach.

In that "church" the men dressed like the general public, but the women were required to wear sleeved dresses with the skirt length below the knees. Slacks, shorts, and makeup were not permitted. The only acceptable jewelry was wedding rings and watches, preferably with plain designs. The women were not allowed to cut their hair, so they wore it up in buns.

TV's and radios were not allowed in homes, though many of us had them. And Christmas was not celebrated, because the Bible does not state the date Jesus was born.

"God's Gift" / J. H. Chappell

In the meetings when someone made their choice to follow Jesus, they dressed properly, read scripture in the service and gave their interpretation of the passage. The Lord's Supper, the bread and wine, was observed each Sunday. I was not sure how they determined when someone was baptized.

When I was nine we moved to southern Oklahoma, about two miles from the Texas border. I felt Jesus call me, so after a morning service I told the lady in whose home the meetings were held, "I want to make my choice to follow Jesus."

"Huh!" she laughed, "You are too young! And besides, you don't even know what it means!" She turned her back to me and talked to another lady who walked up behind her. Embarrassed – I didn't know what to do! I heard them laugh as I went outside until it was time to go home. God called me, and I thought I knew what that meant. It never crossed my mind that a Christian woman would make fun of me. Afraid of further embarrassment, I never mentioned it or pursued God's call for salvation.

"God's Gift" / J. H. Chappell

*"But Jesus said, Suffer little children, and forbid them
not, to come unto me: for of such is the kingdom of heaven."*
(Mat 19:14) *"And whoso shall receive one such little child in
my name receiveth me. But whoso shall offend one of these
little ones which believe in me, it were better for him that a
millstone were hanged about his neck, and that he were
drowned in the depth of the sea."* (Matt 18:5-6)

I began to have nightmares about the workers
(preachers) who unexpectedly visited our home. Afraid they
would catch me dressed in shorts or jeans that I wore around
the house, I hid in the car or outside the house until I found a
way past them to change clothes. I found the nightmares
exhausting, and I became fearful of the church.

A few months later my brothers and I swam in a pond
the color of the Red River. While we played, I got into water
over my head. I couldn't swim. I gently shoved off of the
bottom because it was powdery fine, slimy, red Texas clay.
Too much pressure and my feet would get stuck in the mud. I
pushed off lightly and floated up, as I hoped to make it to the

11

top. When I broke the surface, I gasped for air and splashed to draw attention to myself, then sank to the bottom. Eventually, my brother, Norman, who was eight years older than me, saw me and asked the others if I was drowning. Someone assured him I was playing, but he continued to watch until I surfaced again. Certain I was in trouble, he rescued me. On the bank, Norman grabbed my ankles and shook me upside down like a saltshaker to get the water out of my lungs.

"God, please don't let me die until I'm saved." I heard our days were numbered, but I hoped God would have mercy on me until I belonged to Him.

We moved back to northeastern Oklahoma, into Craig County, after I turned ten. The new house was the prettiest place we had ever lived.

Most of the time I played with my little brother, Chub (Daryl), who was eighteen months younger but bigger than I. We investigated the ranch and walked the two-board, white fence like it was a tightrope. There was a small tree next to the fence that we climbed into and watched Dad heard the cattle past the house. There was added excitement when Dad gathered the bulls.

One day Chub and I were in the tree when two young bulls started to fight below it. Anxiety grew as we felt exposed. Only six feet from the ground, we were too frightened to jump down and run to the house. Frozen with fear, we watched and hoped they would not break through the fence. After several minutes the bulls fought their way toward the center of the pasture where an older bull ran between the two and broke up the fight.

Even though it was one of the most exciting experiences we ever had, after that we watched the bulls from the safety of our screened-in porch.

Then I faced something I feared more than bulls – enrolling in a new school!

Besides an unfamiliar school, we started to attend "church" in a different house. It was the only time we attended meetings in the same town where we went to school. The town was small, and the Baptist church was located next door to the house where the services were held. The street was a dead end street, and the house was located on the entrance corner. I ducked my head when I went inside, because I did not want anyone to know we attended these services.

There weren't any young people in the meetings other than my brothers and me. This home meeting, like the ones to follow, was attended by elderly people.

Each year the church set up canvas tents on a farm for a four-day convention. I often dreaded the conventions, but I got to see my lifelong friend, Joni. I met Joni when I was four and attended services in her home. After we moved I saw her only at special meetings or at conventions.

Joni and I sat together on the canvas bench seats in the meeting tent. The side panels were lowered and the fall air made me feel lighthearted as it blew through the tent. I loved the sound of autumn leaves rustling as a gentle breeze tickled the trees. While workers preached hell, fire and brimstone, I longed for Jesus, but I was comforted by the beautiful days and being with Joni again.

"God's Gift" / J. H. Chappell

As the fourth day wrapped up the convention, Joni was not there. *Susan*, a girl I became friends with in southern Oklahoma, was at the convention. I visited with *Susan* the first three days and wanted to see her once more before the final service. After the lunch break I found *Susan* behind the dining tent. As I approached, I heard her tell some girls I didn't know that I was "worldly" because I wore my dresses above my knees. Dresses were worn below the knees even though fashionable lengths were above the knee or shorter. When the other girls saw me, *Susan* turned around and her face paled with surprise. My face tightened with an expression I could not control as I awkwardly withdrew. Eyes wide with shock, embarrassment made my heart throb as I walked to the abandoned meeting tent. Two workers I had befriended surprised me when they came through the door. I spoke to them and tried to act like nothing was wrong, until one looked at me and walked away, and the other was cold toward me. Overwhelmed, my mind began to race. I felt like I was found guilty at the age of ten and condemned to hell! I knew then, I could never be part of that church. Jesus did not condemn children, and God's love was not there.

"God's Gift" / J. H. Chappell

Confused, I passed by the dining tent and went to our car. The aroma of stew mingled with smoke from the wood stove hung heavy in the air. Someone poured out a basket of apples that sparkled like rubies against the carpet of fall grass. Children and adults alike laughed as they hurried to get one of the gems. I could only wonder w*hat happened. How could such a beautiful day turn out so wrong?*

When I got to the car, my brothers sat with the windows down as they talked and listened to the radio. In defiance of the church's standard of no radios, they listened to escape the people and the church, because they had no interest in either one.

I leaned against the fender and wanted to scream at God, "Why do the men get to dress like everyone else? Was I born just to go to hell?"

I wanted to feel the presence of Jesus and get close to Him like the children in the Bible. Without access to other denominations, life was hopeless. I was empty inside and felt condemned. Emotionally, I spiraled downward.

I felt like a heathen oddity at church, and a Christian oddity at school. I didn't fit in anywhere! Christmas time at

"God's Gift" / J. H. Chappell

school was difficult because each class drew names. We didn't celebrate Christmas, so we were not allowed to participate. Deep inside I yearned for what I missed ...

I recall a time before we were in the church that we celebrated Christmas. When I was four years old, on Christmas Eve, I was told Santa Claus might bring me a new baby doll if I was good, but I had to be asleep when he came. Too excited to sleep, the thought of a new doll flooded my mind. Sleep evaded me as I longed for daylight. *Tomorrow will be Christmas!*

A noise! Could that be Santa? I lay silent and listened. I could hear voices in the living room. After several minutes I climbed out of bed and peeked through the keyhole of the old door. I saw Mom and Dad assembling presents and place them under the tree. Mom picked up a doll and said she would put it in bed with me. I jumped into bed and pretended to sleep. Mom laid the doll next to me then went into the kitchen.

In the darkness I felt the starched dress and plastic shoes. The doll's nylon hair was neatly curled and her eyelids fluttered as I moved them up and down. Like a mother with a

17

newborn baby, I held her hand and felt the tiny fingernails molded into her rubber fingers. I hugged my baby doll until I fell asleep, as I breathed in her fragrance. In the morning I would see what she looked like, even though I knew she was beautiful.

Before I turned five, we moved to another part of the ranch in Osage County. That year for Christmas I got a beautiful bride doll, and Chub got a John Deere pedal tractor. That was the last Christmas we celebrated.

The kids at school asked why we didn't draw names at Christmas. I said we couldn't afford the presents, which was the truth, but not the main reason. After Christmas break someone always asked what I got for Christmas. Anything I got near that time I said was my Christmas present, because I did not want to explain church doctrine. I was always relieved when the New Year came.

I couldn't make friends at school like I had before. My brothers, who were popular, hung out together at the high school and practiced basketball or football. I was lonely for the first time in my life.

18

"God's Gift" / J. H. Chappell

Something changed and I didn't know what it was. I liked our ranch home, but I continually felt like I could cry. One night we built a fire for a wiener roast beyond the front gate. I loved wiener roasts, but as I looked through the screen door at the fire, and listened to the laughter of my family gathered around; I thought, *Why can't I enjoy this* – My heart ached so that I thought I would die. A lump burned in my throat, but the only time I allowed myself to cry was when I was in bed. If I was caught crying, I could never explain what I didn't understand.

I quickly wiped the tears from my eyes and bound out the front door to join the others in laughter. As I made myself laugh to avoid attention, the sad smile drew downward because my heart felt dead within me. I slipped into the darkness until I composed myself then worked my way back into the group.

I had never been sick at heart like I was then, and I wished it would end. Cloudy days and dusk were ominous, and darkness made me feel like someone had stripped my soul.

"God's Gift" / J. H. Chappell

As if Satan taunted me, someone insisted I read a story about a young girl who died of cancer. The story was suggested because they thought I felt sorry for myself. They didn't have a clue that I was seriously depressed and neither did I. Satan had a grip on my heart and when he squeezed it, the fear of death engulfed me.

Our family never discussed our feelings, but neither did anyone else I knew. Even if relatives were nearby, or we had developed deep friendships, I don't think I would have said anything. Joni was my closest friend, and we never discussed our problems.

Mom must have noticed something was wrong, because she arranged for me to spend a week with Joni. Joni lived in town, so we walked to the store to buy candy and did things I could not do on the ranch. It kept my mind occupied, but I got homesick. I knew I would go home soon, so I tried to enjoy the rest of my stay. On Saturday it snowed and Mom could not pick me up until the snow cleared. I tried to cover how homesick I was, but knew my eyes exposed me.

"God's Gift" / J. H. Chappell

After two weeks, I finally made it home. The house looked strangely larger, and I hadn't realized how much I missed my brother, Chub. When I saw him, tears filled my eyes, and I couldn't say a word. Chub must have felt the same, because he held onto the couch like he was introduced to a stranger. Eventually, Mom broke the silence, but it took a while before we were back to our old routine.

When my depression became more than I could bear, I locked myself in the bathroom and quietly cried. I knelt before the commode and poured my heart out to God. I prayed so no one could hear, "God, please lift this from me, I can't take any more! Please give me a spark of happiness. Oh …God! ... Please help me!"

The eight or nine months the depression lingered, nothing could comfort my heart or my soul. I felt like I was dying and no one could stop it. I could not take my life because I would go to hell, and it would destroy my family. The only time I got relief from the torment was in the evening when we were all together and the lights were on in the house. My spirit lifted momentarily as I laughed with the others.

Near bedtime, the horror of depression again flooded my soul because I would be alone in the dark.

We were not an affectionate family, but we loved each other. The year before my brother, Ronny, who was six years older than I, was rushed to the hospital because he had an allergic reaction to a bee sting. The house fell silent with fear, until Mom and Dad brought Ronny home, and we knew he was okay. But that love could not dispel depression.

Since birth, I went to the doctor only once when I was eight years old, to have stitches. Medication was inconceivable, even if it was available. In Matthew 9:20-21, a woman in the Bible had an issue of blood for twelve years. She knew if she touched the hem of Jesus' garment, she would be healed. I was reaching for Jesus, but could not quite touch Him.

Months later I felt sorry for *Susan*, the one who said I was "worldly" at the last convention. Word circulated that *Susan's* dad left her mother for another woman. I was a "daddy's girl," and I couldn't imagine what she had gone through. I thought about the day I visited their home. Her parents took their TV and radio outside, threw them in a heap, and destroyed them. So committed to the church! But he couldn't hold it together – not even for his family. I saw that some adults didn't have it together any more than I did, and you could be accepted into the church, even when your heart wasn't right. We were all in search of God, but I wondered how many would find Him. As hopeless as life looked, there had to be more. I would never give up my search for Jesus, or accept that my ultimate destination was hell!

One Saturday, Ronny's girlfriend asked if I wanted to spend the day with her. I don't remember where we went, but on our way back she checked on her little sister who was at a church camp. The few minutes they talked, my attention was drawn to the service in an open sanctuary. I could feel God's presence and yearned to be part of it, but was silenced as emotion welled up inside me. When we left, I held onto the knowledge that God was out there … beyond our church. And I had to get to Him … somehow!

"God's Gift" / J. H. Chappell

Morning dawned to another day. A cool spring breeze blew through the open window, and the smell of fresh-cut grass tickled my nose. The bird's melodies filled the room and my heart wanted to sing. *Could it be true? Was I happy?* I jumped out of bed and looked outside. The lawn was green, and plush, but empty. I threw on some clothes and ran out the door like a convict freed from prison. I felt like I could fly! *Where is everyone?* I had to find Chub because we had a ranch to investigate. *I'm alive!*

Life was different. According to the church I was not saved, but God lifted the depression. I thanked God repeatedly, as He made my life new and fresh. *"Hath not the potter power over the clay."* (Rom 9:21a) I was a crushed vessel God picked up and started to reshape.

"God, before I die, I hope to see one thing I will know is from You."

CHAPTER THREE

PERSEVERANCE

After my eleventh birthday we moved to Rogers County. I had made friends with a girl there three years earlier, when we lived in Nowata County. She was my age and quickly acquainted me with fellow classmates. In the sixth grade I was as comfortable as my backward personality allowed.

Ever pursued by the Holy Spirit, I hid in the closet or outside when I read the Bible. Comforted by the scriptures and yet convicted, I did not want a sermon on how I should live because salvation seemed beyond my grasp. Regardless, I prayed faithfully every day.

When I was a freshman, Mom's sister and her family came to visit. My aunt, who was of the same faith, told Mom she was too strict because we went to meetings with older people. As sweet as many of them were, I could not dress like they said I should. After Mom gave it some thought, I was allowed to trim my blond hair and wear slacks and a little makeup to school. My goal was not to become the most popular kid in school, although my brothers seemed to be, I was just tired of being an oddball.

I made the basketball team every year, which forced me to become more social. My freshman year was the best ever, but the coach scolded me because I was timid. I heard the word timid so many times that I thought I would scream if I heard it once more. After one practice the coach called me to his office. I didn't know what to expect because I had never been called to anyone's office. He said, "I talked to your Dad the other day." I thought, *this can't be good* as the coach continued. "He said with grass burns on your knees and elbows, you beat Chub one hundred to nothin' when you played tackle football in the yard. Now I know you're not timid. You're afraid you will hurt those girls! Now get out there and play basketball!"

"God's Gift" / J. H. Chappell

The next year the basketball boys did the unimaginable. They voted me the sophomore attendant for the basketball coronation. Without a formal or money to buy one, Dicky's girlfriend let me borrow a formal that fit me perfectly. My neighbor escorted me, and I felt like Cinderella.

Jeanne, Sophomore Attendant, 1970 - 1971

"God's Gift" / J. H. Chappell

Life was good until a dream hit me broadside. It haunted me because I had the same dream before. In my dream a casket was in the foyer outside the doors of the school gym. I was the only one in the building and as I approached the casket my brother, Dicky, sat up and spoke to me. I wanted to tell him to come home, but because of the barrier of death, he couldn't. Even though Dicky was dead, he appeared to be alive.

After I woke up I went through a mourning period for days, as the dream played over in my mind. I had never dealt with the death of anyone close, and could not bear the thought of losing someone in our family. I filed the dream in the back of my mind and focused on other things.

After school I helped Dad train cutting horses that we showed in competition on the weekends. During the summer we gathered the cattle on the ranch and vaccinated, dehorned, wormed and sprayed them for flies. At times we would ship cattle out, and at other times we received new ones onto the ranch.

"God's Gift" / J. H. Chappell

Jeanne on Careless Troubles (Dunny), 1971

While I attended Claremore Junior College, I couldn't get a job for the summer to pay my tuition. I was 19, but was turned down by some businesses because they said I didn't look old enough to drive. I showed them my driver's license, but they were not convinced.

"God's Gift" / J. H. Chappell

Dicky, who had been discharged from the Army, was also in college. He, too, needed money and, as a last resort, he asked if Chub and I would be his hay crew. I knew I was a far cry from my brothers' abilities, but we agreed to haul hay.

I drove the truck in the field, so my job was to feed the bales into the loader. The angled mouth of the loader slid along the ground and pushed the bales into position. The hooked conveyer would lift the bales up the shaft and place them on a platform. If the bales were not retrieved immediately, the next bale would knock it onto the bed of the truck. Dicky and Chub stacked the hay on the truck and I helped unload when we got to the barn.

One day while we loaded the truck, we crossed a beehive in the ground. Dicky yelled, "Go! Go!" I sped up slightly because I thought Dicky had to wait longer than he wanted for the next bale out of the loader. On the other side of the field Dicky tapped on the cab, jumped off the truck, and came to the driver's window. He said, "When I say go – I mean GO! There were bees all over me!"

A few days later I fed the bales into the loader when Dicky yelled, "Go!" I picked up speed as the bed of the old truck creaked and cracked. I zigged and zagged as I got the loader into position to scoop up the next bale. The bales bounced into place like a ball in a pinball machine. Up the loader they went and shot unto the truck like bullets. *They will have to hustle to stack those babies!*

As I got a break between bales, I looked into the side mirror and saw Dicky running behind the truck. It crossed my mind to keep going, but I stopped the truck. I mentally braced myself for the wrath to come, but Dicky didn't say a word as he climbed onto the truck and we continued on as if nothing had happened.

On our best day, we hauled thirty-five tons and that summer we made the money we needed for school.

I continued to live at home while I was in college. The ranch had fourteen thousand acres, and I loved its peaceful atmosphere. Sometimes when I walked near the lake, that was only one hundred yards from the house, I heard someone call my name. When I looked around, there was no one there. I now wonder if God called my name to see if I could hear His voice.

"God's Gift" / J. H. Chappell

Even though I was not saved, God continued to pursue me. My conscience worked overtime, and as I weighed the consequences, I had no desire to smoke, drink, or experiment with drugs. Some of my friends were less inhibited, when they drank – I drove.

When I was twenty-one, my friend, *Sandy,* asked me to go to the lake with her, and her boyfriend, *Buddy,* and his friend, *John.* I hung around with *Sandy* and *Buddy* at rodeos and dances, but was not familiar with *John.* I tried to never get in a position where I was dependant on others, so I told *Sandy,* "I don't think I'll go."

She said, "Oh, come on. There will be about thirty people there and nothing will happen."

I thought they must have arranged for the others we hung around with to meet at the lake. I gave it some thought, but still felt uneasy. I said, "You go ahead. I'll do something else."

"Come on. Nothing will happen!"

"Are you sure it will be all right?"

"It will be okay. You'll see ..."

"God's Gift" / J. H. Chappell

We went to a lake fifty miles away instead of our local lake, and I had no idea where we were. When we got there I asked, "Where are the others?"

Sandy said with a flippant response, "Well, I guess no one else is coming." I knew I had made a dreadful mistake.

That night, *John* tried to rape me. Taken by surprise, I told *John* to stop but he didn't. I yelled, "Stop it!" But he persisted. I thought if I yelled for help, *John* would know I was serious, or *Buddy* would help me. Even that didn't deter him. When *Sandy* and *Buddy* refused to help me, I wanted to rip them all to shreds, so I fought *John* and he finally got the message.

I think I was more upset with *Sandy* than I was with *John*. When I asked why they didn't help me, *Buddy* said he thought it was funny, and *Sandy* didn't say a word. I was enraged! Then as fear swept over me, I felt like I was held hostage by the three of them. Unfamiliar with the area and with no help in sight, I was at their mercy until I got back to my car. I calmed myself and tried not to show fear or anger as I re-evaluated my situation. It was not as much fun as they had hoped, so we were soon on our way.

"God's Gift" / J. H. Chappell

When I got to my car *Sandy* said something, but I never looked back. After I got home, I took a shower and tried to wash away the past. Determined, I would find a new path in life and new friends.

I did not report the assault because I felt like it was three against one. Besides, I should have known better. I did know better, and God tried to warn me, but I ignored His warning. I trusted in someone who was not trustworthy, and did not share my values. I had been betrayed and needed Jesus. He would be my one true friend, and He would never forsake me.

"And ye shall seek me, and find me, when ye shall search for me with all your heart." (Jer. 29:13)

CHAPTER FOUR

FORGIVEN

My brother, Danny, who was two years older than I, invited me to a Baptist church. When I was told Danny had recently been saved, that struck a chord. I desperately wanted what he had, so the next Sunday I was in church. At the end of the service, the pastor invited anyone who felt God's call to come forward. Tears filled my eyes. Unaccustomed to Baptist churches, I was afraid to go forward. A deacon asked me, "Is there anything I can do?"

"No," I said wiping tears from my eyes, "I'm okay."

After the service was over, I released my white-knuckle grip from the pew and left. I cried all the way home because I needed Jesus and didn't have the courage to risk humiliation for Him. After I got home, I called the deacon. He and the pastor met me back at the church, where I asked Jesus to forgive me of my sins and become my Savior.

"God's Gift" / J. H. Chappell

"I say unto you, there is joy in the presence of the angels of God over one sinner that repenteth." (Luke 15:10)

At the age of twenty-two, on June 11, 1978, I surrendered my life to Jesus. I could come forward the next Sunday as a personal testimony of my profession of faith. I left the church with peace I had never known. No longer condemned, I would never have to face hell – EVER!

On July ninth, Danny and I were baptized in Oologah Lake. Redeemed by the blood of Jesus, I never felt cleaner than when I came out of that muddy water.

The day finally came when I could make it on my own, financially. I was able to pay off my new car, my braces, and meet the expense of an apartment. While I filled out the paperwork, the landlady said there were two vacant apartments on the same floor with two single men. I let the information fly as I looked at the apartments. There were four apartments on the second floor and the two vacant apartments were side by side, so I chose the one on the end.

My brothers helped me move and drew the attention of other renters. Dicky threw everything I owned over the second floor rail, to Danny who intercepted them. While Dicky hoisted the couch lengthways over the rail, I carried the breakable dishes up the stairs.

The landlady introduced me to Mike Chappell who lived two apartments down from me. After several months, Mike asked me out. On our first date, Mike, his six-year-old son, Michael, and I went to the National Finals Rodeo. Impressed that I would go on our first date with him and his son, Mike asked me out on a regular basis, and we attended church together.

Mike and I dated three months before he asked me to marry him. We had a new pastor who was in his twenties. When I asked the young pastor if he would perform the wedding ceremony for Mike and me, he said, "I can't marry you, because Mike was married before."

Surprised by his statement, I said, "It's a little late to bring it up now. Why hasn't someone mentioned this before? We love each other and want to get married. Besides, Mike's ex-wife has remarried."

He said, "That doesn't matter; I can't perform the ceremony. Let's pray about it," and he bowed his head and prayed. I didn't want to pray about it because I had prayed about it for months. After he finished, I left.

I told Mike what happened. Faced with adversity, I went to Mike's apartment every night, and together we prayed. We agreed to call the pastor who led me to salvation, and explained the situation to him. He said, "I will speak to the elders of the church, and see if I can perform the ceremony."

I looked in the Bible and read the scriptures that referred to divorce. *"And I say unto you, Whosoever shall put away (divorce) his wife, except it be for fornication (sexual immorality), and shall marry another, commiteth adultery: and whoso marrieth her which is put away doth commit adultery."* (Matt 19:9)

Our plans lined up with the word of God, since Mike's ex-wife remarried. And I believed God brought Mike and me together. But I wondered if I manipulated God's plan.

Late one night, I prayed for assurance that God wanted me to marry Mike. If God showed me it was not His will, I would tell Mike I couldn't marry him. At that moment the phone rang. My former pastor said, "I talked to the elders of the church. They agree, since Mike's ex-wife remarried, Mike is free to marry again and, I can perform the ceremony." I knew that call was God's answer.

I called Mike and told him what the pastor said. Tired of the battle, I asked, "Do you want to get married in two weeks?"

He said, "We can get married tonight if you want!"

With the help of my sisters-in-law and a friend, in two weeks the dresses were sewn, guests were notified, flowers were ordered, the reception was planned and we had the marriage license. Three days before the wedding I panicked! We forgot the blood tests! I called different labs, and it would take five days for a blood test. Finally, I found one lab that could do a blood test in three days!

Mike and I were married in May of 1979, and the wedding was perfect. My brother Dicky brought a wheel barrel and a blanket liner, so Mike could push me down the driveway of the church. When we left the church, we shoved Dicky out of the car as he tried to get in, and we drove through a carwash to wash off the graffiti. I told Mike, "My brothers finally got even with me for what I did to their cars when they got married."

While Mike and I were on our honeymoon, my brothers and sisters-in-law got the keys to our apartments from the landlady. When we turned the corner to the apartment, I said, "It doesn't look right."

Mike asked, "What doesn't look right?"

"The apartment," I echoed, "it doesn't look right."

We rushed up the stairs to my apartment, and our jaws dropped when we looked inside. The apartment was nearly empty. My brothers and sisters-in-law knew we planed to live in my apartment, so they took my furniture, except for the bed, dresser and table to Mike's apartment. After we glanced into my apartment we ran to Mike's and found my furniture stacked in his living room.

Our neighbors said my brothers looked like a colony of ants as they carried my furniture to Mike's apartment.

Mike and I went back to my apartment to assess the damage. It was evident that my family spent time in preparation and execution of their plan of revenge. They had taken my curtains down, except for the ones in the bedroom, and unscrewed every light bulb in the apartment. Tissue hung from the ceiling and doorknobs, and rice and popcorn was strewn throughout the shag carpet.

In the bathroom orange Jell-O four inches deep in the bathtub immediately drew my attention. Shaving cream on the mirror began to melt in our absence. When we looked closer, Saran Wrap was stretched tightly across the stool so it wasn't noticeable when the toilet seat was down. And a fork was wedged under the bar in the tank so it wouldn't flush. I was thankful I used Mike's bathroom.

Our presents were stacked on the table and the top of the wedding cake was placed in the fridge with a new bottle of Champagne. Shaving cream was swooped across each individual egg holder. Since all of my food was taken to Mike's apartment, there was plenty of room for my drain board and dishes to fit in the fridge.

My canned goods stood naked in the cabinet, because the labels were ripped off and put in the dishwasher. We had potluck for the first few meals. After I opened one can I gathered all cans that size, and if the price stamped on them matched, they were labeled accordingly. There were one or two cans that didn't match any others, so I opened them when I felt up to a challenge. Once we discovered the contents inside the can, we planned our meal.

After 10:00 pm the phone rang off the wall. We thought my brothers wanted to give us an old fashioned shivaree, and the calls were to see if we were home. But my brother, Danny, had placed an ad in the Tulsa World that read: "AKC poodle puppies. Leaving town. Must give away. Call after 10:00 pm," and gave both of our phone numbers. I counted thirty-five rings on one call before it stopped. It was weeks before we could plug in the phone. I needed to make a call one day and before I could plug in the phone and dial the number, someone was on the line. I went along with the call, and told the lady we gave all the puppies away. That wouldn't do, she wanted to know what color they were! I didn't want to carry it further so I said, "I just got married and my brothers put that ad in the paper as a joke."

She said, "I don't think that's very funny!"

I said, "If you don't think it's funny, you should be on this side of the line!" and I unplugged the phone again.

"God's Gift" / J. H. Chappell

The next day I went to work, but Mike had the day off so he cleaned the apartment. There was rice in my dresser drawers, shag carpet, and shoes. Months later I found rice stuffed in things I hadn't used in a while, like my sewing box. Mike said, "I don't know what you did to deserve this, but don't EVER do it again!"

Six months later the young pastor apologized because he refused to marry us. He said, "I was wrong."

I said, "I appreciate your apology, but I don't know what to say." God had shown me so much, and I thought of the disaster his advice could have caused.

***

For the last year and a half before the wedding, I was secretary of the Oklahoma Cutting Horse Association. I worked nine hours a day and stayed up until midnight as I updated records, scheduled horse shows and contracted cattle and judges for each event. It kept me exhausted, and it consumed too much time for a newlywed. After I married, I resigned as secretary, and I stopped riding. I focused on God, Mike, Michael and my job.

43

"God's Gift" / J. H. Chappell

The horse I had shown led the Thousand Dollar Novice Class by a large margin. Dad was eligible to enter that class since one of his horses had not won a thousand dollars. From May through December, Dad's horse was the only one who passed what my horse had won. At the awards ceremony I was given the second place buckle. It was an honor to come in second to Dad, because he trained the horses.

THE STALLION

Glistening black stallion, poised,
mouth open, straining hard against the
bit, nostrils flared, neck bowed, muscles
flexed, front legs lifted high in the air.

A child climbs on and hangs on tight.
Silence, as the parents watch. Off
goes the stallion, his stride stretched.
Child wide eyed, they complete the lap.

Here he comes! The stallion stops.
Helping the child off, he cries. The
mighty stallion will never run free
as the carousel circles around.

Jeanne Chappell © May, 2003

44

CHAPTER FIVE

THE HOLY SPIRIT
REVEALS DREAMS

"But this is that which was spoken by the prophet Joel; And it shall come to pass in the last days, saith God, I will pour out of my Spirit upon all flesh: and your sons and your daughters shall prophesy, and your young men shall see visions, and your old men shall dream dreams. And on my servants and on my handmaids I will pour out in those days of my Spirit; and they shall prophesy:" (Acts 2:16-18)

Mike was a Collinsville Police Officer when we met, but went into construction before we married to make more money. Work dwindled, so Mike applied with the Sand Springs Police Department. He was hired in the fall of `79. I worked as a bookkeeper/secretary in Tulsa, so we moved to Tulsa.

"God's Gift" / J. H. Chappell

Mike's six-year-old son, Michael, grew so attached to me that he wanted to live with us. He told Mike, "You know, Jeanne is my mother in God's way." Within two years we were granted custody of Michael. After four years, Michael's mother asked if I wanted to adopt him. She signed the papers, and I adopted Michael as my own.

During that time, God prepared Mike and me for events to come. I didn't know about spiritual gifts or prophetic gifts from God, but I knew God had spoken to me. God gave me dreams and visions, but at times I was not sure how He spoke to me.

I worked days and Mike worked nights, so he left for work before I got home. Every night before bedtime, Mike called to tell me goodnight and fill me in on the day's events.

There was a new school under construction in the area Mike patrolled. The officers checked the school nightly for burglars and vandals, because it was vandalized before. The grounds at the school were rough, and the dirt road around the property was laden with potholes.

Mike called one night at midnight and woke me up. He said, "Jeanne, I have to go to the hospital. I hurt my back."

I asked, "What did you do, fall in a hole again?"

He replied, "Yes. I fell in a hole. How did you know?"

Irritated, I said, "If you don't quit falling in those holes, you will get shot!"

Mike said, defending himself, "This is the first time I fell in one of the holes."

I insisted, "It is not! You checked on the school for burglars during the night, and fell in a hole!"

Mike said, confused, "Jeanne, that's the way it happened. But this was the first time I fell in one of the holes." He added, "You must have just dreamed it. If you ever dream I get shot, call me!"

A few months later, Mike had comp-time on the books, so he asked for the night off. I was in my ninth month of pregnancy with our daughter, and Mike felt he should stay home.

That night because the department was short handed, Detective Darland worked patrol. When he pulled up to the school, something looked out of place. As Detective Darland investigated, a suspect stepped out of the shadows and shot him point-blank in the back. The impact of the .357 magnum knocked Detective Darland several feet forward and to the ground. Even with a bulletproof vest, it took a few weeks for the internal bruises to heal.

When Mike heard Detective Darland was shot at the school, Mike remembered what I told him months earlier. Mike realized he could have been the one shot if he had gone to work, because he always checked the school on his shift.

God kept Mike home that night, but we could not grasp all we were spared. Our baby girl, Shawna, would be born in three weeks, and God knew we could not deal with such a crisis. In turn, I had to wonder why God allowed Detective Darland to be there at that time.

A year and a half later, on December 23, 1981, I called Mike from work like I did every day. I told Mike I loved him and asked him to be careful. When I got home, Michael, Shawna and I had a typical evening. It was two days before Christmas, so they were excited about their Christmas presents. Michael played with the neighbors, and after dinner and their baths, Michael and Shawna were fast asleep. At

9:30, I decided to get ready for bed when the phone rang. It was Mike. He said, "Jeanne, are you sitting down?"

I said, "No. What did you do, get shot?"

"Yes."

"Are you okay?"

"I'm alright."

"No, I really want to know; are you okay?"

"I'm fine." Mike said, "One of the dispatchers wanted to call, but I thought I should tell you."

"I'm glad you did," as I tried to digest what I just heard. "What happened?"

"I responded to an armed robbery at the Family Market, and was shot with a .357. The bullet hit me in the chest, but did not penetrate my bulletproof vest. An inch higher, it would have missed the vest. They took me to the medical clinic and checked me over. I pulled my shirttail out of my pants and almost fainted when I heard the .38 round hit the floor. That's when reality hit!" Mike added, "Don't try to drive. They will send a dispatcher to pick you up. Can you get someone to watch Michael and Shawna?"

"I'll get one of the neighbors."

"God's Gift" / J. H. Chappell

"See you when you get here."

When I hung up the phone, my first instinct was panic. My feet wanted to run to different rooms in the house and do everything all at once. But I made myself stand there and think rationally. *What do I need to do?* I went across the street and explained everything to our neighbor. After he agreed to sit with Michael and Shawna, I ran back to the house. *What now?* I changed clothes and brushed my hair. *What else? My purse! Think! Think!* ... I couldn't think of anything else.

Our neighbor arrived minutes before the dispatcher pulled in the driveway. On the way to the police department, she assured me that Mike was fine. I know we talked, but I don't remember much about the conversation or the trip.

This is a combination of the reports written: On 12-23-81, at approximately 1947 hours (7:47 pm), Sgt. Chappell and Cpl. Ecker were dispatched to an armed robbery, at the Family Market in Sand Springs. Shots were fired, and the suspect who wore a ski mask, was still inside the store.

Upon arrival Sgt. Chappell and Cpl. Ecker approached the front door of the store. The suspect had his left arm around a man's neck with a sawed-off shotgun in that hand, while the pistol he held in his right hand was pointed at the man's head. Cpl. Ecker yelled for the suspect to freeze, as Sgt. Chappell told everyone to get down. The suspect pushed the man away and shot at the officers. Cpl. Ecker fired two or three rounds and Sgt. Chappell fired one.

Sgt. Chappell then moved to a position to cover the citizens in the store. When the suspect shot again, Cpl. Ecker fired two more rounds. The suspect was hit in the right leg and a bullet grazed his head above the right eye.

Sgt. Chappell was between the pop box and front checkout counter inside the store, when the suspect shot at him. Sgt. Chappell returned fire. Sgt. Chappell then rushed the citizens out of the store through the front door.

Crouched in front of aisle two, Cpl. Ecker dropped five spent rounds and one unfired round as he reloaded his revolver. Sgt. Chappell yelled that the suspect was behind Cpl. Ecker in the freezer aisle. Cpl. Ecker rolled forward around aisle two.

The suspect fired a round at Sgt. Chappell, which struck him on the inside top corner of his right shirt pocket.

Sgt. Chappell returned fire and hit the suspect in the right elbow. Sgt. Chappell yelled, "I've been hit!" Unaware, he pushed the transmit button on his radio and it went out over the air. Cpl. Ecker told Sgt. Chappell to fall down, as Cpl. Ecker climbed over a store display and was able to cover the suspect. The suspect yelled and threw the revolver and sawed-off shotgun into the main aisle. Sgt. Chappell covered the suspect and advised Cpl. Ecker that the suspect had given up. Cpl. Ecker ran around the aisle to the suspect, kicked the weapons away, and they cuffed him.

Sgt. Chappell requested a detective and an ambulance over the radio. When the medics arrived to treat the suspect's injuries, the suspect advised Cpl. Ecker that he was on PCP.

After the scene was secured and turned over to Detective Darland, Sgt. Chappell walked out of the store, unbuttoned his shirt, and said, "Thank God and Second Chance, I'm alive!" as his knees buckled and he collapsed in the parking lot. Sgt. Chappell was taken to a nearby clinic.

At the police department Mike's adrenalin was so high he could not sit still. Hours later Mike continued to pace the floor and talked extremely fast as he recapped every detail of the gunfight. After the reports were written, the detective thought Mike should go home and rest.

Mike's adrenalin was still very high, and he talked non-stop as I drove. When we got home, Mike told our neighbor what happened. I went into the kitchen to get a drink of water, and my mind went blank. I looked at our cabinets and could not remember where we kept our glasses. I opened cabinets until I found them.

When Mike's adrenalin crashed, he broke down and wept because he realized he could have been killed.

Early the next morning we told our nine-year-old son, Michael, that Mike was shot the night before. The news instantly made Michael sick, a reaction we had not anticipated, but we assured him that his dad was okay.

On Christmas day, a local TV station wanted to do a human-interest story, since Mike was shot so close to Christmas. When the reporter arrived to interview us, she was disappointed that we had opened our presents and cleaned up the wrapping paper.

"God's Gift" / J. H. Chappell

During the interview, after Mike told her what happened the night of the shooting, she asked if I worried when Mike was on duty. The only time I worried about Mike was if I felt something was wrong. Mike wore his bulletproof vest, and I prayed for God's protection. That was all we could do. The rest was up to God. Michael said he was glad his dad was okay, but Shawna, who was eighteen months old, wasn't aware of what happened.

As the days passed, I got nauseated when Mike retold the story with each phone call. It helped Mike to talk about it, but I was thankful when the calls stopped.

Mike was off work for one week, due to a blood clot caused from the impact of the bullet. He returned to work on New Year's Eve on the midnight shift.

Mike was given his choice of a new vest from the Second Chance Company, because Mike wore one of their vests when he was shot. If someone was shot or stabbed while they wore a Second Chance vest and survived, Second Chance replaced their damaged vest. Mike was also given a small check for the use of his story in their magazine. Mike was their 249th "save". As I write this, Mike still wears a Second Chance vest on duty.

Mike, shot in the line of duty, December 23, 1981

Months later, we all laughed that Cpl. Ecker told Mike to fall down when Mike said he was shot. In Ecker's defense he told Mike to fall down because he thought Mike was trying to draw the suspect out. Cpl. Ecker was a Green Beret while he served in Vietnam, and was active reserve in Special Forces at the time of the gunfight. That combined with his sense of humor and how fast one can think and talk during an adrenalin rush, we were not surprised at the conversation or activity that took place in only a few minutes.

God's protection, a bulletproof vest and Special Forces! What more could you ask for in a gunfight?

The man who shot Mike was sentenced to 225 years for what he did that night: (75 years for armed robbery and 150 years for shooting with intent to kill.) An additional 15-year sentence was added because he violated his parole. His parole was revoked, so he had to finish his original sentence before he started the 240 years.

On December 19, 1981, three days before Mike was shot, he applied for the Oklahoma Highway Patrol Academy. Through months of physical competition and tests that O.H.P. required, Mike was nearly impossible to live with. As Mike waited for word that he had advanced to the next step, I questioned whether our marriage would survive.

"God's Gift" / J. H. Chappell

Mike grew more anxious when weeks passed without word from the department. If applicants did not make it, they were never notified. To make matters worse, those who were accepted were notified on different days.

We went out to eat one afternoon, and when we walked in the door the phone was ringing. Mike answered it, and a lady from personnel asked, "Are you Mike Chappell?"

"Yes."

"I am with personnel in Oklahoma City. I want to verify that you are still interested in the patrol academy."

"Yes, I am."

"I was going to let the phone ring one more time, then take your name off the list."

"Leave my name on the list! I'm interested!"

Anxiety set in, and Mike thought he had washed out if some got word ahead of him. Mike heard the background checks were in progress, and wanted to call one of his references to see if anyone from O.H.P. had contacted him.

I said, "I talked to him the other day. He told me a trooper came out but only stayed five minutes."

Mike replied, "They usually stay about two hours."

"God's Gift" / J. H. Chappell

Two days later Mike called him. When Mike hung up the phone, he said with a stunned look, "You were right. A trooper came out and only stayed five minutes." Mike added, "Jeanne, the trooper didn't come out until today!"

The academy was to start in three weeks ... Nothing!

Every Saturday, we hoped and prayed for a letter. When the letter didn't come, it was a rough weekend.

Two weeks before the academy started, we clung to our last thread of hope. Several received letters of acceptance, and if Mike didn't receive a letter Saturday, he didn't make the academy. We were at the door when the mailman made his round. The mailman handed Mike a letter and said, "Well, open it so we can see if you made it!"

"I guess we owe you that, after the grief we have given you." Mike scanned the letter, "I MADE IT!"

The mailman congratulated Mike and left with a smile as he finished his route.

Mike resigned his police position, and we bought and marked the supplies listed in the letter.

"God's Gift" / J. H. Chappell

May 1, 1982, was the first day of the 39th O.H.P. Academy. Nervous cadets with their families signed in and waited for instructions. The cadets were taken one direction and family members were taken another. I attended orientation for the spouses, where we were told about the cadets, "The next sixteen weeks we are going to screw up their brains, then send them home to you."

I thought, *Great!*

We were instructed not to call the cadets during the academy, or expect to hear from them for three weeks. I told Mike to focus 100% on the academy, and I would handle everything at home. But I didn't want to hear a word about how I handled things while he was gone. He agreed.

I headed home and Mike started four months of sleepless nights, physical endurance and patrol training.

After I got home I received a call from a cadet's wife. *Liz* asked, "Have you heard from Mike?"

"No. They aren't supposed to call for three weeks."

"Okay. Bye." and she hung up.

I felt a bit uneasy but continued with my chores.

"*God's Gift*" / J. H. Chappell

A few hours later I got a call from another cadet's wife. *Joy* asked, "Have you heard from Mike tonight?"

"No. They aren't allowed to call for three weeks."

She said, "*Liz* called. Her husband walked out of the academy after four hours."

I asked, "Why?"

She said, "I don't know. I hoped you knew." Abruptly she added, "I will talk to you tomorrow," and hung up.

I thought, *What is going on down there?*

After a restless night's sleep, I called *Joy* the next morning. *Joy* also picked her husband up the night before. He walked out after seven hours. When I asked why, *Joy* said she was not sure, and we never found out.

I felt isolated. Even though I didn't know *Joy* or *Liz*, I was familiar with their husbands because Mike mentioned them many times. I had their phone numbers in case I needed to talk to someone while Mike was in the academy; someone who could relate to our situation. In one night I was on my own. Frantic, I wrote Mike a letter.

Mike drove us crazy with his mood swings and irritability prior to his acceptance; we were not ready to deal with worse, if he didn't make it through. If Mike walked out, he would have to deal with *my* mood swings. Mike wrote me back, "Don't worry, I'm not going to walk out. I worked too hard to get here." I felt better but would not be at ease until graduation.

After three weeks, we got to see each other for four hours. The rest of the time, they were released Friday afternoon, and had to report back by noon on Sunday. Mike's time at home was used to catch up on rest since they were only allowed to sleep one to three hours a night. While Mike slept, I did his laundry and got his clothes ready to go back.

Mike said on the third day while he did pushups, he saw a vision of himself in full uniform in a patrol car. Mike hurt his arm the second day, so he held onto the vision to get him through. Around the twelfth of May, which was our third wedding anniversary, I felt Mike was hurt, and I was reluctant to open his next letter. When I did, sure enough, there it was! He hurt both arms, and the medic couldn't help him. Mike failed one physical training test but didn't give up.

Halfway through the academy, the cadets were required to pass the same tests it took to get in, only the requirements were more strict – body fat, mile and a half run, pushups – if the cadets could not pass, they were dismisscd. By the grace of God, Mike passed. The ninth week the cadets were allowed more sleep, and we had one full weekend together.

Mike's shoulders were in bad shape, and he didn't know if he could make it to the end. I knew he would make it because I, too, had a vision where Mike drove a patrol car onto the driveway, stepped out in full uniform, and stood beside it.

I told Mom and Dad about Mike's shoulders. Dad said he had some tiny pills the chiropractor gave him for bursitis, that lubricated the joints. Dad gave them to Mike, and after a couple of days Mike was as good as new, so Dad kept Mike supplied for the rest of the academy. God provided what we needed when we needed it. But after Mike graduated the pills were no longer manufactured.

After Michael and Shawna were asleep I wallpapered and painted until midnight. I got the house ready to sell, in case Mike was assigned a position where we had to move.

**Jeanne, Shawna, Mike and Michael
Mike's O.H.P. graduation, 1982**

Two weeks before graduation the cadets were given
their assignments. Mike was assigned Tulsa, so we didn't
have to move. Out of eighty-five cadets, eighteen walked out
or were forced to leave. Of the sixty-seven graduates
approximately one-third were given assignments near their

63

homes, one-third requested assignments where they could move and one-third were assigned areas that required a move.

Determined, we all made it through. Twenty pounds lighter Mike graduated from the academy two days before Shawna's second birthday, in August of 1982.

Now we can breathe easy for a while.

"I am on probation for one year."

Maybe we can relax in a year –

A year later, on October 5, 1983, my co-workers said a trooper was shot near Sapulpa. They were worried about Mike because his territory butted up to that area. Mike sometimes worked with the two that patrolled that section because they were out of the same academy. But Mike was on his days off, so I knew he was safe.

I went home for lunch and found Mike pacing the floor because he didn't know which trooper was shot. He was reluctant to call dispatch because a manhunt was top priority. I could not get Leon Bench off of my mind. When the news came on, it showed Leon's car number. Mike lost it when they showed the bullet holes in Leon's patrol car and a pool of blood on the ground. On his days off and helpless, Mike asked his supervisor if he could go back to work because he needed to stay busy. His Lieutenant said he could.

Twenty-four hours a day two troopers stood at parade rest, at the head and foot of Leon's casket. Mike was one of the two asked to stand guard the night before the funeral and through the service. I was concerned whether he could hold up that long. Honored to serve his brother one last time, wild horses couldn't pull Mike away from his fallen partner's side.

On October 26, 1984, I woke up nauseous. I told Mike, "I dreamed your Troop Commander called and asked if I was sitting down. I knew you were okay because you were outside working on your car. He wanted to know if our twenty-five-dollar check was covered, since we changed banks. I told him that it was and asked what happened? He named a trooper from the Tulsa area, and said he had been shot and killed in the line of duty."

O.H.P. had a twenty-five dollar plan. All participants wrote checks that were held until a trooper on the plan passed away, then the checks were cashed and the money was given to the spouse or next of kin.

That morning, which was Friday, I made sure the check was covered because I worked at the bank. Afraid my dream would distract the trooper and cause him to do something careless – we didn't tell him.

On Saturday, the twenty-seventh, we got word that Guy Nalley was shot and killed on a traffic stop in western Oklahoma. He, too, was out of Mike's academy that graduated two years earlier. Because the one named was not the one shot, it confirmed that the dream was to prepare us and was never meant as a warning for the trooper.

On September 4, 1988, I had another significant dream. In my dream, I saw troopers calmly visit as they stood around a closed casket. I didn't know how the trooper died, but I knew he was not killed in the line of duty.

On the tenth Keith Kuwitsky, a trooper who lived ten miles from us was killed in a pickup wreck on Highway 75.

As tragic as the news always was, God did soften the blow with each dream.

CHAPTER SIX

BEHIND THE BADGE
BEATS A HEART FOR JESUS

After Shawna was born, Mike insisted I continue to work outside the home. We were in debt, and we could not afford for me to quit. Regardless, I felt the need to stay home and raise the children. Guilt ate at me while I worked, because others raised Shawna at daycare. After Shawna started school the guilt let up slightly, but I longed to be there when she and Michael got home from school. Then one day Shawna said something that set me free. Mike, Michael, and Shawna had teased me, when Shawna said, "Yeah, go to work and make some more money."

I said, "It doesn't bother you when I go to work?"

"No. We have a good time while you're gone."

We could not afford for me to stay home, so I looked to a career and retirement. Disgusted with salaries women made, I was determined to find a job where men and women were paid the same.

I applied with Troop "N" of the Oklahoma Highway Patrol for a civilian position. For two and a half years as a new position opened, I learned that it was filled from within the department, so I decided on a different route.

Shawna turned nine and Michael would be seventeen. We discussed how they would feel if I became a police officer. Mike worked days and got off at 2:00 in the afternoon. If I worked nights, Mike would be there.

I applied with Troop "R" of the Oklahoma Highway Patrol for a state police position. It was a requirement to work one year as a probationary officer before you could transfer to another division. I was hired on October 9, 1989, so I resigned my position at the bank. Mike was concerned about my new career, but I got a sixty percent raise in pay. If I had to work, I would go where the money was.

I was CLEET certified within six months. The Counsel on Law Enforcement Education Training certifies and trains officers around the state, whose departments are not large enough to conduct their own academies.

Jeanne's police graduation, 1990

I started eight weeks of police training at the same time our son, Michael, was in eight weeks of basic training in the Navy.

Michael on leave from the Gulf War, 1991

After I became a police officer, my brother, Dicky and I were on common ground for the first time in our lives. He stopped by occasionally and visited while we were both on duty. We discussed our jobs and what we had encountered.

"God's Gift" / J. H. Chappell

Other Tulsa Police officers I visited with told me stories about Dicky. If I have the story correct, one young officer said they responded to a burglary call, but their search came up empty. The building had a flat roof, and he asked Dicky who would search the roof. Dicky said, "You're the rookie. You will," and before he could ask how he would get up there, Dicky picked him up and threw him on top of the building.

I don't remember if it was the same officer that told me – "When Dicky was in a fight, even if he fought five guys, I learned to stay back until he said to cuff them. Dicky didn't look at uniforms; he decked whoever was in front of him." The officer added, "I thought he would kill me in one fight – he hit me so hard!"

Dicky's first K-9, Ronny, must have learned a lot from Dicky. Ronny loved the pursuit and didn't look at uniforms either. If Ronny was pursuing a suspect, and the suspect stopped; before Dicky could call him off, Ronny would bite the next person he saw running, as fellow officers found out.

Dicky loved a good fight because it tested his strength. Growing up, our brother Ronny's, gentle nature irritated

Dicky who was less patient. Occasionally, they would come to blows, but I don't think Dicky ever stirred Ronny to his full potential because Mom or Dad stopped the fight and neither conceded that the other was stronger.

While Dicky and I talked, he had to laugh when he told me the worst beating he ever took was from a ninety-eight pound girl. He was taking her to jail when she slipped out of the cuffs and fought him while he drove down Interstate 244 in Tulsa. She tried to choke him with one arm and had her other arm wrapped around his head, which covered his eyes. He said, "It was all I could do to fight her and get my car to the side of the road without wrecking." Laughing he added, "I thought she would beat me to death before I got her under control!"

Before Dicky went back on patrol, I hugged him and said, "I love you."

Dicky nervously looked around and said, "Good grief," as he hated being sentimental, "someone will probably complain on us."

"I don't care –" I said, laughing at him, "Let them complain." I always hoped it would not be our last hug …

"God's Gift" / J. H. Chappell

As a police officer, I came across bad situations and drew unstable people like a magnet. It became so bizarre; I had a personal distress code on the radio in case a call for backup would escalate the situation. Many times when I called for backup my hand-held radio didn't work, so I was on my own. Mike's concern for my safety was elevated.

I thought if we got out of debt, I could stay home. So I decided to transfer to the Lake Patrol instead of Troop "N". It had additional dangers, but it paid more. The equipment was better, and the schedule was less rigid.

From the magnetic attraction I had for trouble, Mike thought it was too dangerous for me to patrol a lake alone. He had a valid point, but it would knock off two hours on my drive to and from work, that could be better spent at home. If I was assigned the lake near our home, I could check out for lunch at the house. I pursued the transfer with a passion. I kind of left it up to God. I prayed, "God, if You don't want me on the Lake Patrol, keep me off. Because I will do all I can to get transferred."

I passed the merit test, and I was certified as a lifeguard and a search and recovery diver to meet the requirements. I was number one on the register statewide, and no women had been hired full-time by that division … but the Lake Patrol didn't transfer anyone in, or hire a single person during the four years that I was number one on the list.

We moved from Tulsa to Rogers County in the fall of '92. I joined a church close to home, and within a year the church split. I continued to attend for a while, but the mood in the congregation was strained and lifeless. I wanted to find a church where I could seek the face of God.

I visited the First Baptist Church in Talala, which was a very small, country church. Raised in that area, it was likely I knew some of the people. The moment I walked through the doors, I knew I was home! I found what I had searched for because I felt the presence of God!

After I joined the church in February of '94, God spoke to my heart continually through the Holy Spirit. I knew the transfer to the Lake Patrol was not God's will, because the weekends were their busiest days. If I worked Sundays, Shawna and I would lose the fellowship we built with Jesus and our church family.

"God's Gift" / J. H. Chappell

My health deteriorated, as if overnight my knees gave out. The public was more volatile, and the fights had taken their toll on my body. I could no longer meet the demands of police work, and the Lake Patrol required more than I could give. I reconsidered the transfer to Troop "N", as a civilian employee. There were no weekend or night shifts, and theoretically it was less dangerous. Plus, I would not have to physically fight anyone.

I gained a wealth of knowledge from the five years I pursued the transfer to the Lake Patrol. I saw God lock doors that should have blown wide open to keep me in His will, and He rolled out the red carpet, so to speak, when I was on the path He laid before me.

As a police officer, I tried to do things God's way. One of my partners, Don, was an ordained Pentecostal Minister. When we patrolled together, we discussed what God revealed to us about our families and our jobs.

As if we read each other's minds, Don and I recognized that the bizarre situations had ceased for the last couple of months. I felt like God had me in a protective bubble. Then for no reason, late in my shift, I got extremely sick for one hour. The pain was so intense it made me double over. After the pain passed, I was fine. I went to the doctor and after a series of tests; he told me I needed to have a hysterectomy. After four months of battling the insurance company, I was scheduled for surgery.

On August 1, 1994, I went into the hospital and the surgery went well. When I asked the doctor what all was wrong, he named off several things he had written down and then said, "There wasn't anything that wasn't wrong."

On the third day after my surgery, I closed my eyes to go to sleep when I sensed something was not right. Through my eyelids, I saw a bright light appear in the room. I opened my eyes, but the room was so bright it looked empty. To my right, I heard Satan yell at me. His voice had a dreadful, guttural sound – a deep, raspy, bass sound that a human voice could not duplicate. I could not understand what he said or why he was there. I said the only thing that came to mind, "Get thee behind me, Satan," and closed my eyes to go to sleep. When the bright light appeared the second time, I opened my eyes and again Satan screamed at me. I echoed,

"God's Gift" / J. H. Chappell

"Get thee behind me, Satan!" As I tried to go to sleep the third time, it happened once more. Satan's voice was louder than ever. Finally, I said, "Get thee behind me, Satan! I'm going to sleep, and you can't get me! I'm not yours! I belong to Jesus!" I was then able to go to sleep.

I believe the bright light was an angel that stood between Satan and me. The angel was so bright I could not look in that direction. I could never comprehend the magnitude of God's love until that day.

"For I am persuaded, that neither death, nor life, nor angels, nor principalities, nor powers, nor things present, nor things to come, Nor height, nor depth, nor any creature, shall be able to separate us from the love of God, which is in Christ Jesus our Lord." (Rom 8:38-39) Saved by the blood of Jesus, nothing could separate me from Him ... Nothing!

I could not understand Satan. It was not the voice of my Master. *"My sheep hear my voice, and I know them, and they follow me:"* (John 10:27)

I could feel God's protection in the room, but I was amazed at the extent Satan goes to torment a Christian.

77

"God's Gift" / J. H. Chappell

I told Shawna about what had happened and that I was in the room by myself. I didn't think I was ever alone because I had a roommate. Shawna said, "Mom, on the third day they moved that girl out of your room."

When I left the hospital I felt good, but within two weeks I had to walk doubled over. I thought I pulled a stomach muscle when I sneezed. Mike told me to stand up straight and stretch the muscle. But I couldn't. A small spot started to protrude, and it burned like it was on fire. The doctor told me to come to his office immediately, where he drained off 200 cc's of bacteria. The inner stitches abscessed because they did not dissolve. The physician opened the incision two more times, each more than the last. Finally, he opened it to its original length, and removed the inner stitches. The four-inch incision that went to the depth of my stomach muscle was left to heal without stitches, tape or staples.

My body fought the infection, as I woke up drenched in sweat. Twenty-three nights in a row, Mike helped me change soaked gowns, and when I shivered uncontrollably, he piled on the covers. At times Mike or Shawna used the hair dryer to blow heat under the covers, to warm me and dry me.

After thirteen weeks, I went back to work. Before my surgery I was sick and my hormones were out of balance, so everything set me off. Because I experienced God's love and peace after my surgery, I was different. When I went back to work, I was extremely calm. As officers deliberately tried to stir me up, nothing fazed me. A couple of months later one of my partners, who couldn't take it any longer, said, "Okay, I know you're a clone, where is the real Jeanne?"

I said, "Gone," as I questioned whether I had enough fight to handle explosive situations.

Don and I relied on each other more than ever. But it wouldn't be long before we parted ways. Attrition depleted our staff, and I would be transferred soon.

Five weeks before my transfer, we received a call about a woman whose abused child was taken from her. On the way to see her caseworker, the woman said she would go to jail that day. The woman was verbally abusive, so her caseworker called us. As Don and I escorted her out of the building, she asked, "What if I don't leave?"

I said, "We'll arrest you."

In an instant, she hit me in the chest and the lower part of my throat. My vest took the impact to the chest, and because of adrenalin, I did not feel the blow to my throat. I threw her into the wall, and she grabbed my shirt collar with her left hand. It was during the winter, and our winter uniform buttoned to the top with a clip-on tie. I maintained an airway, as I tried to loosen her grip that held my collar like a vice. From her tremendous strength it was obvious she was on some kind of drug, which we later learned was PCP.

I kneed her in the gut over and over, but nothing Don or I tried fazed her. After several minutes, I thought if we took her to the floor, she would let go since our natural reflex when we fall is to catch ourselves. I planned to sweep her legs so she would fall away from the wall and land on her back between us. If she let go of my collar, I could roll her over with her arm and have her in an arm bar. If she didn't let go, she would pull me down on top of her. Don's report said she kicked, which tripped him. He must have fallen into her at the moment I swept her legs, which sent her momentum my direction. I hit the floor hard, flat on my back. She crashed down on my chest and left leg, with her left hand on my throat. Don fell on top of her, and her right elbow went into his rib cage, which caused his ribs to separate and puncture his liver and stomach. Don lay stunned for a few seconds. As I started to black out, I saw her reach for Don's pistol with her right hand. I got them off of me enough to breathe. I yelled, "She's after your gun!" which threw Don back into action.

A caseworker asked if we wanted his help. We both managed, "Yes!"

Together, it was all we could do to cuff her. She continued to kick violently, so we cuffed her ankles. After she calmed down, we jailed her.

On the way to jail, she apologized over and over for trying to hurt me. Then she asked, "What are you charging me with?"

I said, "Two counts of assault and battery on a police officer and resisting arrest."

She bluntly said to me, "I didn't do anything to him! I was after you!"

"God's Gift" / J. H. Chappell

The woman pled guilty to one count of felony assault and battery on a police officer and was sentenced to five years. We could not prove intent for Don's injuries.

I sustained trauma to my neck, but Don broke a bone in his right hand besides the damage to his ribs, liver and stomach. Don was off work, and as complications arose, his return was further away. Our department pressured Don to come back, but light duty was not available.

Before the fight Don worked part time for a security company to make additional money. After Don was injured, the security company offered him a full-time, supervisory position out of state. It paid more, and Don could sit behind a desk, but he was not sure if he should take it. Don thought God was leading him in that direction, because his brother, who was a Gospel minister, lived there and needed family nearby. Don's wife and daughters were so excited that they were ready to leave, with or without him. Finally, Don resigned his position and moved his family.

Don and I talked about how God worked out the details. If Don was not injured, he would never have quit his job and moved out of state. On the other hand, if I were injured, Troop "N" would have denied my transfer. God used our circumstances to change our direction.

I lost contact with Don until April of 2003, when he told me he had cancer of the pancreas and wasn't given much time. Don said his mother and twin sister, who passed away years ago, were by his bedside one night. Don's twin sister touched his hand and his mother said, "The supper table is almost ready, and I will wait for you. Don, have peace in your heart because it won't be long before we are together." She added, "Ear hath not heard or eyes can't behold the beauty there. It is like the Bible teaches, but more – so much more than your earthly body can bear. You have to be in the spirit to see it all."

***

I tested for Troop "N", and was number one on the register for a location four hours from home. If I were stationed there it would not be for long. Shawna turned fifteen, and I felt God wanted me to stay close to home. As the time drew near, the Troop Commander asked if I would like to stay in the Tulsa area. I gladly accepted the Tulsa assignment and was transferred on October 9, 1995.

My co-workers were great, but I missed Don. I felt alone until someone started to talk about God, and then I saw that Christians surrounded me. As I got acquainted with my new work family, I had never met anyone who went to the depth of my co-worker, Jeanie, to know Jesus. She asked profound questions and explained in depth how she felt as she described what she saw. She took on everything and everybody with a fierce conviction like a Chihuahua who takes on a Saint Bernard. From the passion she held for Jesus in conversation, The Holy Spirit bubbled over which made Jesus real. Jeanie was exactly what I needed in my life!

God began to use me in a new way, as He put messages on my heart for Jeanie. The first letter I wrote, she said, "This note is from God."

"What makes you say that?"

"Because it contains things I was told years ago. Things you would never have known on your own."

Goose bumps went over me like a caress from God.

"God's Gift" / J. H. Chappell

In December of 1995, God put it on my heart to start a spiritual journal. As I wrote what God showed me, I felt like I was tied by an umbilical cord to heaven. At times I thought my heart would explode because God's Spirit was so strong. "Lord, please don't back away – not even if it kills me!"

I was in prayer one morning, when Mike asked, "What are you doing?" When I heard his distant voice, I felt something supernatural pull from me like a hand from a latex glove. Numb from its tranquil presence, I was oblivious to everything. It took a moment before I located Mike standing about ten feet from me. Frustration hit because something precious was taken from me, and I was thrust back into the daily grind. I wanted to lash out, but knew I shouldn't. I finally answered, "Praying." Mike left so I could continue my time with God, but my focus was shattered. I battled emotions, until I held tight to the memory of when The Holy Spirit consumed me.

"God's Gift" / J. H. Chappell

THE HAND OF GOD

The hand of God is ever present
In our daily lives.
Sometimes in miraculous ways,
Sometimes unrecognized.

To find God we must seek Him.
He won't come against our will.
Lest I miss what He is doing.
Quiet my heart. Be still.

Jeanne Chappell © March, 2005

86

CHAPTER SEVEN

OFFICER DOWN!
ANGELS ON THE SCENE

"For we wrestle not against flesh and blood, but against principalities, against powers, against the rulers of the darkness of this world, against spiritual wickedness in high places." (Eph 6:12)

On Sunday, June 9, 1996, I made a copy of Revelation 21:10 through 22:2, the description of the holy Jerusalem descending out of heaven from God. I felt the need to picture what my future home in heaven looked like.

[Later I learned that Dicky's killer stole a car on that day, and had stolen some guns within the past three days.]

On Monday, the tenth, everyone at work was on edge. Unable to identify the problem, it was unusual because we were all testy at the same time. We had dealt with spiritual

87

warfare before. But you can't pinpoint what it's about until you are in the storm. I tried to find peace, so I read the scripture I copied Sunday for my co-worker, Jeanie.

Mid-afternoon, God put it on my heart to buy Bibles and other supplies for my brothers. I focused on the items I would purchase, which calmed me. On the way home I stopped by a Christian bookstore and bought what I needed. The clerk asked if I wanted names inscribed on the Bibles. I said, "No. They are for my brothers, and I don't know which brother I will give one to first."

I thought I would give a set to Dicky and Daryl (Chub) the next time I saw them, and before Mom and Dad's fiftieth wedding anniversary in August, I would buy a set for Norman and Ronny, who lived out of state. At home I separated the Bibles and materials so they were readily available when my brothers visited.

[Because of the alcohol reported in the gunman's blood, he drank that day, and it was reasoned that he also conspired to commit an armed robbery.]

"God's Gift" / J. H. Chappell

Like two runaway trains on a collision course – the battle between good and evil would collide in an alley, with Dicky, Steve, and Dino, caught in the middle.

At midnight we received the call that Dicky had been shot. To my knowledge these are the events of that night:

Dicky and Steve (another K-9 officer with the Tulsa Police Department) responded to an armed robbery at a fast food restaurant. When the suspect fled the restaurant he wrecked his car. Witnesses saw the suspect run toward an alley in downtown Tulsa. A transient from the streets, the suspect was probably familiar with the area.

As Dicky entered the alley with his dog, Dino, Dicky was shot in the leg with twenty-gauge birdshot, which knocked him down. The gunman turned on Steve, who was also in the alley, and shot him in the leg. The gunman turned back to Dicky and shot him in the right side.

During the gunfight Dino attacked the gunman, then ran back to check on Dicky ... back and forth. Dicky emptied his semi-automatic weapon, while Steve and three backup officers fired at the gunman with Dino in the middle. An angel must have covered Dino because there wasn't a scratch on him. If there was an angel with Dino, I know there were probably several with Dicky and Steve.

The gunman died of a fatal gunshot wound.

After the firearms fell silent, Dino, geared for battle, stood guard over his fallen master. Trained to protect, Dino refused to surrender Dicky to medics or fellow police officers. In the midst of chaos, the commands Dino heard that called him away from Dicky went against his instincts. Devoted to protect Dicky but realizing that something was terribly wrong, Dino was eventually coaxed away so Dicky could receive medical attention.

After Dicky passed away early the next morning, my sister-in-law, Ann (Dicky's wife), asked me to assist her with Dicky's funeral arrangements. The burden was lightened when the Garnett Church of Christ was offered for the funeral service, and the Moore Funeral Home and Floral Haven Cemetery donated their services. There were few decisions to make.

"God's Gift" / J. H. Chappell

That afternoon, I told my brother, Ronny, who drove up from Texas, "It bothers me because I don't know if Dicky was saved. I hope you will hear what the letter of salvation told you, and I hope you will be saved."

Exhausted, I walked next door to my home from Mom and Dad's. The letter was the last communication I had with Dicky. I thought *I should have pursued Dicky more about salvation.* In my spirit I heard, "I told you to write the letters, I did not tell you to pursue him." Reassured, guilt left me.

The next morning, on the twelfth, we went to the funeral home to see Dicky. We tried to grasp that he was really gone, but inwardly hoped it was just a bad dream. We stayed for hours, because we could not bring ourselves to walk away.

As we dealt with our grief, I mentally took in the scene around me. I saw the officers who stood at parade rest at the head and foot of Dicky's casket. I remembered when Mike stood beside his fallen partner's casket and how hard that duty was. I thought of how close my husband, Mike, and I came to being put in that position when we were in our twenties. Again, I thanked God that Mike was not fatally wounded when he was shot. But, I could not fully grasp the extent of how difficult it could have been, until the memorial services were over and I saw the toll that Dicky's death took on our family.

As the images burned in my mind, I was continually drawn to the expression on Dicky's face. To me, he had a sassy little smile on his face and looked peaceful. I knew in my heart that Dicky was with Jesus.

When we left the funeral home, my brother, Daryl, and I felt the need to visit Steve in the hospital – the other officer who was shot in the gunfight. We encouraged Steve to get well and not to focus on *"what if"* or *"if I had only ..."* We had a good visit which broke some of the tension.

Later that afternoon my husband, Mike, and my brother, Ronny and I visited in our home. Mike left the room briefly, when The Holy Spirit prompted me to ask Ronny if he wanted to be saved. I was tense from all that had happened the last few days, and I felt animated. Things happened so fast that I felt like I was on a runaway horse. But I knew that missed opportunities may never surface twice, so I squeezed out the words. When Ronny, with a surprised look said, "Yes," I involuntarily took a quick breath. I fought the urge to panic and said to myself, "We can do this." With our hearts pounding, we knelt in the living room as I led Ronny in prayer. After Ronny asked Jesus to forgive his sins and come into his heart, we thanked God for his salvation.

When Ronny and I told our brothers the good news, Ronny said, "When Dicky was killed it made me think of my own mortality. I remembered things we did growing up, and it's a wonder any of us survived. Dicky and I were the two strongest in the family, and after I saw how fast you can be taken, I knew I needed to receive Jesus as my Savior."

I was unable to sleep that night, because I mourned for Dicky and rejoiced over Ronny's salvation. *"Blessed are they that mourn: for they shall be comforted."* (Mat 5:4) *"Rejoice, because your names are written in heaven."* (Luke 10:20b)

Flags flew at half-mast, and people statewide drove with their headlights on in Dicky's honor. Friday, on the way to the funeral, a Tulsa police car led the procession of four family limousines. A police helicopter flew in front of the patrol car until we got to Tulsa, where we were joined by a second helicopter. Motorcycles joined in and escorted us as patrol cars blocked every street. As we neared the Garnett Church of Christ in Tulsa where the service was held, we were forced to use the oncoming lanes, because traffic was jammed due to the funeral. The church parking lot was full of police cars while the overflow parked on the lawn.

Bagpipes played as we followed Dicky's casket into the church. Honor Guard made up of police officers from departments throughout the state lined the sidewalk.

Dicky's casket was displayed in the center of the large rotunda. The first song played had an angelic sound. Then "Daddy's Hands" and a beautiful song about Jesus Christ were sung. There were two poems read: one was "When God Created Fathers" by Erma Bombeck, and the other spoke of Dicky's sacrifice and said goodbye. Letters were read that children wrote to Dicky and his first K-9, Officer Ronny. The Mayor, the District Attorney, and the Chief of Police spoke before the Tulsa Police Chaplain gave the eulogy.

"God's Gift" / J. H. Chappell

Ronny and Dino, Dicky's K-9's, were then brought onto the platform to give tribute to Dicky. Ronny was very weak, but Dino stood proud. The Honor Guard folded the flag on Dicky's casket, saluted him, and then placed the folded flag back on the casket. The church was cleared so we could say our final farewells.

During the service, I felt *there is something different about this funeral.* Several said they sensed something different about Dicky's funeral but didn't know what it was, so they started to pray. God's presence was so strong I could feel it. Then I heard in my spirit, "Watch what I do with this."

When Mike and I saw Dicky for the last time, Dicky's smile immediately drew me in. The Tulsa Police Chaplain must have seen I was captivated, so he touched my arm. Suddenly aware of my surroundings, I looked at him. He said, "Jeanne, you will see him again in heaven."

"I know." I was surprised that for a moment, I was unaware of everything but the expression on Dicky's face.

Bagpipes played as we followed the casket through the Honor Guard back to the limousines. Police helicopters and motorcycles in formation, escorted us to the cemetery as police cars followed by the hundreds. Men, women, and children lined the street. Tears streamed down the faces of many as some held their hands over their hearts. Those with hats, placed them over their hearts as the procession passed, while others sat in their cars with their headlights on.

The newspaper reported twenty-eight hundred people attended the service, of which over one thousand were police officers. Later it was estimated around six thousand people attended, counting the ones who lined the streets. The funeral service was televised so an undetermined number watched it on TV.

At the cemetery Dicky was honored by the Canine Corp.; the Horse Patrol led the rider-less horse; the many officers of the Honor Guard stood at attention; bagpipes and taps were played; the helicopters did a fly-by; and a twenty-one gun salute set the K-9's to wail for a fallen master, led by Dino who remembered Monday night.

"God's Gift" / J. H. Chappell

DICKY 1951 – 1996 and **DINO** 1991 – 2005

Andy's Fine Portraits,
4213 S. Rockford, Tulsa, OK 74105

"God's Gift" / J. H. Chappell

Dicky's funeral motorcade

Tulsa World, Tulsa, OK.
Chief Photographer, Rabbit Hare.
Stephen Pingry / Tulsa World.

"God's Gift" / J. H. Chappell

The Fraternal Order of Police held a wake in Dicky's honor after the funeral. Dicky could not have been honored more than he was that day.

That evening, Ronny was baptized at our Church – a perfect end to a stressful day. Ronny was nervous so we took only a few family members with us. It fell into place like the letter of salvation stated in February. You can be baptized with only a few family members present.

When Ronny went back to Texas, I sent a Bible and other materials with him. I was led to buy the Bibles on Monday because God knew Ronny would be there Tuesday. I saw that week was not about death or murder. It was about God's plan. It was Dicky's time to go, and God let him die a hero!

One of the news clips had shown Dicky sitting up as they loaded him into the ambulance. From what we could see, Dicky didn't show signs of fear, or anger. He looked good. I originally understood Dicky was unconscious.

"God's Gift" / J. H. Chappell

My pastor said even when a person is unconscious they know what is happening. Others agreed. The only way I could relate to that was when I had foot surgery. As I came out from under the anesthesia, I heard a girl's distant screams. After a while I became annoyed and wished she would shut up! Then I heard the nurses talking. A moment later I heard my doctor tell me to open my eyes. I was awake, but my eyelids were too heavy to open, and I couldn't speak. I continued to struggle and got them to budge. Then I realized that the screams were from me. I had an allergic reaction to the anesthetic, so the doctor was afraid to give me pain medication. My body cried out, but my conscious spirit was not aware of the pain.

God assured me that Dicky had time to ask for forgiveness after he was shot. And, hopefully, his spirit didn't experience the anguish his body must have felt.

Dicky's neighbor said ten days before the gunfight, Dicky said he would get shot someday. She said, "Don't talk like that!"

He said, "No. I really think someday I'll get it."

"God's Gift" / J. H. Chappell

"LORD, make me to know mine end, and the measure of my days, what it is; that I may know how frail I am." (Psalm 39:4)

God's presence must have overwhelmed Dicky for him to make such an intimate statement. From what God revealed, Dicky must have known it was more than a possibility that he would get shot, and wanted us to know that he was aware of it. Dicky was probably afraid family could not handle what he had to say, but knew his neighbor would have the courage to tell us, if, and when it happened. I was thankful that God had warned Dicky.

I saw how God prepared Dicky for salvation and death; prepared Ronny for salvation; and prepared me to witness to my brothers and lead Ronny to the Lord. I wondered if the reason Dicky didn't die instantly was because Jesus needed a little more time with him to save his soul, or perhaps God needed time to get us in place. Was Steve shot to show he could have been killed, but it was not his time? Was Dicky shot twice to show it was no accident? Did Dino come out of the fight without a scratch to show it was a miracle and God was in control?

101

"God's Gift" / J. H. Chappell

Dicky died eighteen years to the day, from the day I was saved. I felt God showed me that Dicky was saved that day!

From what we were told or could piece together, Dicky died approximately seven hours after he was shot, and his blood volume was replaced seven times. In the Bible, the number seven represents, sacrifice, forgiveness, purification, consecration, perfection, rest, reward, abundance, judgment and completeness. Because of the very nature of Jesus, He made all of those possible through the events of that night.

A couple of weeks after Dicky's funeral, I went to his grave. I heard in my spirit, "Why do you look for the living among the dead? He is not here." *"O grave, where is thy victory?"* (1 Cor 15:55b) Dicky's body was there, but his spirit was with God. *"But God will redeem my soul from the power of the grave: for he shall receive me."* (Psalm 49:15)

I recalled what I thought were weird dreams as a teenager, were actually steeped in meaning. The week of Dicky's death, I partially understood what God tried to show me years earlier. But it took an additional nine years before I understood the entire dream.

In my dreams *a casket was in the foyer, outside the doors of the school gym.* Nearly three decades later I understood. The casket was outside the gym because it was not Dicky's time; otherwise it would have been in a service. It also meant that Dicky's funeral would be large. Funerals too large for area churches were usually held in school gymnasiums. The church where Dicky's funeral was held was extraordinary because it held thousands.

As I approached the casket in my dreams, *Dicky sat up and spoke to me.* God not only prepared me for Dicky's death, but He used the expression on Dicky's face to speak to me and let me know that Dicky was at peace. In the dreams *I was the only one in the building besides Dicky.* While I stood next to Dicky's casket, captivated by his expression, I was unaware of everyone but the two of us.

I wanted to tell Dicky to come home in my dreams, *but because of the barrier of death, he couldn't. Even though he was dead, he appeared alive.* God tried to tell me as a teenager, that Dicky would live after his death. Dicky's body was dead, but his spirit was alive in the presence of God. And, because of the barrier of death – Dicky went home.

We were doing a study of "Experiencing God" by Henry Blackaby and Claude King at church. After the funeral our study asked: "How can we show our love for God?" *"Be willing to lay down your life for your brothers."* (John 15:13) Dicky laid down his life for his brothers. But even if we are not asked to lay down our lives, we are asked to put our lives aside to witness to others.

Three weeks later God gave me a message I thought was beautifully stated in the workbook. Jesus was talking to Mary and Martha about their brother, Lazarus, whom Jesus raised from the dead. But when I read it, He spoke to me.

"You are exactly right. If I had come, your brother would not have died. You know that I could have healed him, because you have seen Me heal many, many times. If I had come when you asked Me to, I would have healed him. But, you would have never known any more about Me than you already know. I knew that you were ready for a greater revelation of Me than you have ever known in your life. I

"God's Gift" / J. H. Chappell

wanted you to come to know that I am the resurrection and the life. My refusal and My silence was not rejection. It was an opportunity for Me to disclose to you more of Me than you have ever known."

(Experiencing God by Henry Blackaby and Claude King)

***

To my knowledge, the one who shot Dicky was a twenty-one-year-old transient with a history of mental illness. He was diagnosed with schizophrenia, but refused treatment. He had a criminal record but no major offenses until he stole a car, a gun and was involved in an armed robbery that resulted in Dicky's murder.

Ironically, the gunman's father was a K-9 Officer, who was forced to retire after he was shot in the line of duty. I had to wonder; *What thoughts of his father, if any, crossed the gunman's mind when he saw K-9 officers enter the alley, and when he pulled the trigger?*

105

"God's Gift" / J. H. Chappell

As I drove to work one day, God spoke to my heart and said, "You are no better than the one who shot Dicky." Then it hit me. God loved him as much as God loves me. Because I received Jesus as my Savior, God had mercy on me and blessed me.

God said to pray for our enemies. So I prayed for Dicky's killer. I didn't consider him an enemy, because I didn't think of him one-way or the other. Furthermore, I don't believe prayers for the dead can change their fate, but I felt led to pray for him. *"None of them can by any means redeem his brother, nor give to God a ransom for him: (For the redemption of their soul is precious, and it ceaseth forever:)"* (Psalm 49:7-8) *"And beside all this, between us and you there is a great gulf fixed: so that they which would pass from hence to you cannot; neither can they pass to us, that would come from thence."* (Luke 16:26)

Only God knew where Dicky's killer was in eternity, and he was there forever! Maybe it was a test to see if I had truly forgiven him. If prayers for the dead had no benefit, hate toward the dead was less beneficial. Regardless, I prayed for him and let God sort it out. I believe because of that prayer, I experienced one of the most profound blessings I have ever experienced.

Three weeks after Dicky's death, on July 2nd, I was asleep when something awoke me. Mike rolled over on his right side and faced away from me. I looked up and saw a right hand with a bright, golden glow suspended in air beside the foot of the bed. I don't know if the hand was larger than normal, or if the golden glow made it appear larger. Afraid to blink for fear it would disappear, I never took my eyes off of it. There was something in the palm of the hand that was bright gold, shaped like a small book. It was a gift. As the hand lowered toward me, it passed over me and moved above Mike. It descended and went through Mike, leaving the gift. Eventually, God would reveal what it meant.

After everyone went home, and the awards and memorial services were over, I was able to relax. *"Come unto me, all ye that labour and are heavy laden and I will give you rest."* (Matt 11:28) For three days, every time I closed my eyes I saw Dicky standing outside a gate to heaven. Dicky stood alone with a smile from ear to ear. Heaven was not for me to see, so God let me see Dicky outside the gate, to confirm all He had shown me.

CHAPTER EIGHT

JESUS, MY SOLACE, MY PROVIDER

"And it shall come to pass, when I bring a cloud over the earth, that the bow shall be seen in the cloud: And I will remember my covenant, which is between me and you and every living creature of all flesh; and the waters shall no more become a flood to destroy all flesh. And the bow shall be in the cloud; and I will look upon it, that I may remember the everlasting covenant between God and every living creature of all flesh that is upon the earth." (Gen 9:14-16)

Six weeks after Dicky's death while I was on vacation, my co-worker, Lisa, called. She said Jeanie's stepfather, Jim, who was a retired O.H.P. Captain, passed away on August 5, 1996. My co-worker, Jeanie, held Jim in such high esteem … she would go to Jim for answers before she went to Jesus. Jeanie placed Jim on a pedestal in her heart, which no other man could reach. Forced to rely on Jesus or lose her sanity, Jesus would become Lord of her life.

On August seventh, Mike and I attended Jim's funeral. Also that day, my sister-in-law, Ann, had Dicky's first K-9, Ronny, put down because of cancer. High on emotion I had to be there for Jeanie.

At the graveside service everyone tried to get underneath the canopy. The sweltering heat and the lack of air, were suffocating. At one point I backed away to get a breath of air. I looked up and expected to see the sun beating down on us, but saw puffy white clouds. Before I left the cemetery, I told Jeanie to look at the beautiful clouds God placed in the sky.

As we drove home there was a small black cloud hovering overhead, and I thought *that must be Jeanie's little black cloud.* Later in the evening, there was a rainbow in the clouds. It wasn't in front or below the clouds, it was woven into the clouds. We had never seen anything like it. I took a picture, but I could only faintly see the colors.

"God's Gift" / J. H. Chappell

When I showed Jeanie her little black cloud, I said the rainbow was a sign that Jim was okay. Part of one cloud was shaped like a white dove, and the cloud itself looked like it had a lace fringe around the edge.

After I showed Jeanie the pictures, she remembered a card that a nine-year-old boy sent. On the front of the card a white dove flew from the palm of a hand that glowed, or was surrounded by glittering light. When I read the card, I couldn't believe my eyes. It read: *"Let your heart take wing, for there are brighter days ahead. Even the darkest night turns rosy at dawn and the most threatening clouds give birth to rainbows. Peace be with you always."*

[L-IMAGE GRAPHICS, by J.O.T.T. Graphics 1992, Written by Anne K. Shelly]

Jeanie said that eighteen years earlier when she was in her early twenties, Jim had a heart attack, and his heart stopped beating. In ICU, after Jim was revived, Jeanie went in to see him. There was a bright glow that looked like shimmering gold dust in the room. When Jeanie looked at Jim, she was forced to rub her eyes because the bright glow hurt them.

111

"God's Gift" / J. H. Chappell

After Jim's funeral, Jeanie's mother, Helen, said when Jim was in the hospital, he saw a hand with a golden glow around it. The hand opened and released a white dove.

After we put the card, the story and the pictures together, we were in awe of how God comforted our hearts. I could only wonder *how many times had He tried to comfort us, and we missed His message, His signs or His presence?*

God had shown us a rosebud, but it came into full bloom four years later when Jeanie's mother, Helen Snider, was led to write a book about her life with Jim. Helen worked on the book for three years, but no cover was suitable. Nearing completion, Helen prayed for God to show her the cover. Seven years after Jim's death, Helen was drawn to a box of keepsakes. Packed in the box was the picture of the dove shaped cloud that I took on the day of Jim's funeral. Helen knew it was the cover for her book, "The Years of Tears and His Glory."

***

I desired a closer walk with God, so I would fast one day each week, and God revealed something personal each time.

"God's Gift" / J. H. Chappell

Our study at church asked what we were praying for that was "God-sized". I had never prayed like that or trusted God in that way. The study showed us that God is waiting to do things for us and through us, that only He can do. So I asked God to do something "God-sized" in my life.

On October eleventh, 1996, the Holy Spirit revealed the meaning of the vision of the right hand that glowed. As the hand lowered toward me, it passed over me and moved above Mike. It descended and went through Mike and left the gift. The Holy Spirit showed me that my spiritual journal was a gift from God, to Mike, through me.

As I let close friends read my journal, several said I should write a book. My reply was, "The only way I will make my journals into a book, is if God tells me to do so!"

The next day, on October twelfth, I knew God wanted me to write a book. The Holy Spirit showed me the cover, the title, how to make chapters, and a computer He would provide. The book in the palm of the hand meant the book would be small. As Mike watches what God does through this book, God will touch his heart as never before, and it will be God's gift to him.

"God's Gift" / J. H. Chappell

I remembered a picture I took of a cloud, before Dicky was shot. The cloud looked like a right hand that held the sun in the palm, and light shined between the fingers. I had the picture enlarged, and it was ready the day Dicky died.

The Holy Spirit led me to the verse from Isaiah 41:1, *"Fear thou not; for I am with thee: be not dismayed; for I am thy God: I will strengthen thee; yea, I will help thee; yea, I will uphold thee with the right hand of my righteousness."* I believe that was the ultimate message of the two right hands. God would uphold me through the publication of this book, and uphold this book to reach those He intended.

***

In 1999 it was time to leave the department. God wanted me somewhere else. As I began to get sick, Mike and I saw that it would be impossible for me to stay. God confirmed He wanted me to leave when Mike said, "If the legislators pass our pay raise, you can retire. Your job takes too much out of you, and it's not worth it."

After four years in Troop "N", and ten years with the department; God provided a way for me to retire on November 1, 1999, which was my heart's desire.

"God's Gift" / J. H. Chappell

I told Mike, "No matter what happens after I retire, I want at least one year to stay home and be renewed." One year later, illness struck our family ...

***

LIFE'S BETRAYAL

His wrinkled face gives way to fear as Alzheimer's encroaches on his mind. In his prime he backed down from no man, now he's a child again. Follows his wife like a child his mother, not sure of anything anymore.

Taste of salt from the tears he sheds, reminiscent of sweat from his brow. He used to smell of a hard day's work, toiled from sunup till sundown. The odor of cattle, hay, or a barn, reminds him – it has been too long.

Fragrance of leather, horses and rain, bring his senses to life. Horse shows and dogs, time in the saddle – memories of an old ranch hand. He would love to ride the range once more, hear the wind whistle through the trees.

Looks out the window a young man he recalls, breaking horses and building fence. The world hides as the sun sets low, he sees an old man look in. The face seems strange, a lone tear rolls down the furrows of a weather worn face.

In the tapestry of life the colors faded, and the threads have all grown bare. The wisdom and strength Dad once possessed, slipped away like a subtle betrayal. Someday he will ride over the last sunset, and feel like a young man again.

(Jeanne Chappell © May, 2003)

115

"God's Gift" / J. H. Chappell

***

Shawna ready for an FFA meeting, 1996

Shawna graduated from high school in 1998, and she married after she turned eighteen. A year and a half later she gave birth to their first child, Destiny. Their second child,

116

Justin, was born a year and three weeks after Destiny's birth, in April of 2001. Justin immediately developed pneumonia after birth, and was transported by Life Flight to a neonatal unit in Tulsa. The first few days while he was in the hospital, complications arose. I knew we were not to worry because God was in control, but it upset me. Then the Holy Spirit reminded me of a vision I had years earlier.

When Shawna was little, she said several times, "When I get married I want to have a baby boy." When Shawna was thirteen or fourteen, I had a vision of a little boy with curly, blond hair. The little boy dressed in overalls, was about eighteen months old and he leaned nonchalantly against our couch. I knew in my heart he was Shawna's little boy.

While Justin was in intensive care, the vision I had more than six years earlier, assured me that he would be fine. Justin would get well, or he would never be eighteen months old. Justin was released a few days later and developed into a beautiful, healthy, little boy with curly, blond hair.

Justin and Destiny, 2002

***

Over the years I saw what we lacked as children, we pursued with a passion as adults. Daryl (Chub) was the only one who didn't remember celebrating Christmas as a child. As an adult, he made a point to decorate for every holiday, and hung thousands of lights at Christmas. In the year 2000 Daryl didn't put up as many Christmas lights as before.

In March of 2001 Daryl was admitted into the hospital and diagnosed with cancer of the lungs and lymph-nodes. I asked Daryl, because he was in such bad shape, if he had asked Jesus to be his Savior? He said, "Yes," but could say little more. Daryl's vocal cords were paralyzed, so he could hardly talk loud enough to be heard. He improved slightly and was released from the hospital.

Over the next year Daryl endured radiation as the cancer spread throughout his body. On April 7, 2002, while I visited Daryl at home, he said, "I know I'm going to die."

I asked, "Does that scare you?"

"A little," he added, "I want to be saved again."

If you were saved once – you are saved. But for Daryl's peace of mind, we prayed together. Daryl understood that Jesus went to the cross to save us from our sins. So Daryl confessed he was a sinner, and asked Jesus to forgive him. Daryl said he felt better after he asked Jesus to become his Savior, and I explained that he was saved the first time he called on Jesus, because Jesus knew his heart. But because of

119

the way we were taught growing up, Daryl needed assurance of his salvation. We went on to talk about what the Bible says about heaven.

Daryl said, "I had a dream a few days ago, that was quite pretty. I was on the adjustable bed and I saw a bright glow on the loveseat. It was so bright I couldn't see what was inside the light."

I said, "It was probably an angel."

"I hadn't thought of that."

"Ministering angels are probably all around this room."

He said with a bit of a laugh, "They probably are."

On the ninth of April, Daryl wanted me to tell him once more about passing over into heaven. After I told him again what the Bible says about heaven, Daryl said he was ready to go. But his concern was then directed to his twenty-three-year-old daughter, Dana, who was the pride of his life and all that kept him going. I could not relate to what Dana endured on a daily basis, as she through her abundant love, cared for her dad's every need. Even if someone were in the same situation at that age, the circumstances would never be the same, so no one this side of heaven could fully relate to what she had endured. As I watched how she handled their daily lives and each obstacle they faced, it was nothing short of miraculous.

Daryl had me promise that I would talk to Dana about salvation before I left. My gut wrenched because I hated to put one more decision on her. Dana's gentle nature reminded me of Daryl's, and I wasn't sure how much more she could stand. She had already dealt with more than seasoned adults could tolerate, things she may never be able to talk about to anyone but God Himself – but I had promised Daryl.

That afternoon Dana asked Jesus to forgive her sins and come into her heart. When Daryl was told, he was truly at peace because the one he loved more than life itself, was sealed by the blood of Jesus. Daryl and Dana had a connection that few fathers and daughters experience. Now his impending death could only separate them for a time because in heaven, they would be together for all eternity!

Daryl maintained his sweet spirit while he battled cancer, and went to be with the Lord on April 18, 2002. The same age as our brother Dicky, Daryl was forty-five years old.

"God's Gift" / J. H. Chappell

I thought about the contrast between Dicky and Daryl's deaths, even though there were many similarities in their personal lives. Daryl slipped quietly through life with little notice, and left the same way, as less than two hundred people attended his funeral. Because of the nature of Dicky's job and his death, he was on the news many times and thousands attended his funeral while possibly more watched it on TV. Still, both brothers had the same impact on our family. Dicky went unexpectedly and very quickly, while Daryl was given a year to prepare. We asked questions and said goodbye to Daryl before he left. Even though I got answers to the same questions I had for Dicky, the answers were revealed in a different manner.

REBIRTH

Family by his bedside, he knows in his languished heart,
Smile breaks through as pain enfolds him, he is going home.
Like a cocoon gives way to life, a butterfly writhes free.
Vanquished worm's spirit flies, gives way to virgin form.

Christ Jesus like a beacon calls His child home.
His spirit slips from flesh and bone, rebirths a glorified form.
Enemies, fear, pain and sorrow forever left behind
Into the presence of Jesus, Who pales the noonday sun.

Jeanne Chappell © May, 2003

CHAPTER NINE

THE JOURNEY'S END

Because of my police background, I recognized details I would have otherwise missed, as God revealed more about Dicky's shooting.

Shortly after Dicky died, I felt Dicky was shot on the date, that was his badge number. I could not shake the feeling, so I called the chief's office. They said Dicky's badge number was 109. I could not understand why I felt it was 106.

After I retired, more than four years after Dicky's death, an officer sent a tape home with Mike so we could hear Dicky's voice. The officer was from a small town near Tulsa, and was in a pursuit in 1995. Dicky, with his K-9, assisted the officer when the assailant fled on foot.

I listened to the tape and noticed Dicky's voice resembled Daryl's. Then I heard it! Something the Tulsa Police Chief said at Dicky's funeral, but I had forgotten. Dicky's call number was King 106! He was shot on the date corresponding with his number, 10-6, the tenth day of June! I thought w*hy is this important for me to know?* Jesus, the King of Kings, was in control of every intricate detail of that night! There wasn't anything left to chance! Dicky was in the palm of God's hand then ... but in His presence today!

Like the parables Jesus told, the true meaning was veiled by something else. Only the ones who belonged to God understood the message. Dicky's call number was veiled by his badge number. It was not for everyone to see or understand, much like the night Dicky was shot. If you did not look for God in the circumstances of that night and the weeks that followed, you would never see God in them.

As the years have passed, Dicky's memory is still as vivid today as it was then. I remember his mannerisms, and the way he laughed after he teased someone. Dicky twisted his hair and smiled as he stared into space, thinking about who knows what. The memories have become a part of me, and I feel Dicky is always near.

I have handled the normal grieving process very well, but not the memorial services that followed or the annual memorial services. The officers who have died in the line of duty deserve to be honored. But it's hard to memorialize someone yearly, whom you have spent your entire childhood and most of your teenage years with. He was one of my big brothers, and it's hard to tell where they end, and I begin. We all became part of each other over the years, and were unaware that it happened.

I also find it hard, because it brings my focus back to the day Dicky was shot and the day he died. God has shown me, the day Dicky died was not the end – it was the beginning. I often think of how it must be with Dicky in the presence of Jesus – in the full glory of God!

I will never forget the officers we have known, who lost their lives in the line of duty. But it's not the same when one of the officers is your brother. I will never forget Dicky and neither will anyone else in our family. But it hurts too much to feel like we are burying him once more. Maybe one day I will attend the memorial services, but for now, they will have to wait. I am thankful to those who honor Dicky, whether in a service or in their hearts. Dicky wasn't perfect, but he was a good man and was once nominated for Police Officer of the Year because he was a good officer. He, like the others, deserves to be honored for his sacrifice. But for now, the services may have to go on without family members who wish they could attend, but can't bring themselves to face it once more.

I thought about our paths in life. I accepted Jesus as my Savior while Dicky was in the police academy. Eighteen years later, Dicky died on the date I was saved. God started to weave our lives together for His purpose before we were born. I wondered why God saved us from death so many times in our youth, but saw how He used our lives to fulfill His plan years later. Separation from Dicky and Daryl is only temporary, because I will see them again in heaven.

I think about the officers in the gunfight, and those who helped us through Dicky's death. I would love to hug all of them once more, and those who carry fond thoughts of Dicky and our family in their hearts. Maybe I will – someday.

CHAPTER TEN

CONCLUSION

***

WHAT I WOULD LOVE

To go to heaven like Elijah.
With chariots of fire, taken up in a whirlwind
because he walked with God.

Have the anointing God gave Elisha.
God's spirit so strong, after he died
his bones revived the dead.

Humble myself like Mary Magdalene.
Washed Jesus' feet with her tears,
and dried them with her hair.

Speak with God like Moses.
Stand barefoot on holy ground,
as God's glory radiated off of his face.

Love others like Jesus
Gave His life for us, and didn't recant
in spite of all He faced.

"God's Gift" / J. H. Chappell

Have a vision like Jacob.
Angels descend and ascend the ladder to heaven,
then wrestle with God and win.

Be obedient like Noah.
Worked 120 years to build the ark, prepared
for a flood when rain had never fallen.

Have the faith of Abraham.
Willing to sacrifice his son when commanded,
but trust God to provide another way.

Repent like David.
Be considered someone after God's own heart,
and repent of the calamities he instigated.

To stand on faith.
That my children and grandchildren will follow Jesus,
and know He is the one who guides them.

Jeanne Chappell © May, 2003

I saw our son, Michael, accept Jesus as his Savior at the age of nine, and our daughter, Shawna, accept Jesus before she turned nine. God called them at the age He called me.

As a child I longed for God, and hoped to see one thing that was from Him. My life appeared dull until The

130

Holy Spirit had me write down what He did. Through the whirlwind of events, I cannot write all God has shown me. I wonder how many have gone to their graves and never saw what God did in their lives?

I can relate to the Apostle Paul when he said in Philippians 1:23-24, *"For I am in a strait betwixt two, having a desire to depart, and to be with Christ; which is far better: Nevertheless to abide in the flesh is more needful for you."* I long to be with Jesus, but I know God wants me to teach my children and grandchildren to recognize His voice. As long as I am here on earth, I hope to reach many souls for God's eternal kingdom.

When I get homesick to see the full glory of God in Jesus, I try to picture what heaven is like. The glory of God is so bright, there will be no darkness. Not even a shadow. (Rev 21:1-27, 22:1-5).

We will be more alive than ever, because we will have glorified bodies that will never grow old. In heaven we will serve Jesus and worship Him. There will be no more tears, no sorrow, no death, no fear and no more pain.

"God's Gift" / J. H. Chappell

I long to see the holy Jerusalem descend out of heaven from God, full of His glory, with its light like a precious jasper stone, clear as crystal. I try to imagine what a crystal city, fifteen-hundred miles wide, long, and high, would look like. Its great street, like the city, is pure gold and looks like clear glass. The twelve gates are each made of one huge pearl. The city's twelve colored foundations of the wall are garnished with precious stones. The Lamb of God is the temple therein, and His glory shines forever. The pure river of the water of life, clear as crystal, proceeds out of the throne of God and of the Lamb. In the middle of the street of gold, and on either side of the river, is the tree of life. It bares twelve kinds of fruit, a different one every month. And its leaves are for the healing of nations.

I want to see the Old Testament Saints, New Testament Saints, and the present day Saints who have gone on – of which Dicky and Daryl will be among. I long to see God's host of angels and the place Jesus has prepared for me. Jesus said, *"In my Father's house are many mansions: if it were not so, I would have told you. I go to prepare a place for you. And if I go and prepare a place for you, I will come again, and receive you unto myself; that where I am, there ye may be also."* (John 14:2-3)

When God calls us home – our spirit will not taste death. The moment our bodies die on this side of life, if we are saved, our soul will immediately be in the presence of Jesus. (II Cor 5:8)

If you don't know Jesus as your personal Savior, please take this time to ask Him to forgive you of your sins and to come into your heart. If you are not sure of your salvation, ask forgiveness of any sin in your life, and ask Jesus to give you assurance that you are saved by His blood. Then begin your walk with Him.

Seek the face of God by opening your eyes, open your Bible, open your heart and pray. Jesus is waiting for you. Ask God to reveal Himself to you, and teach you how to recognize Him. It will be the most wonderful thing you will ever do. Ask in Jesus' name – and believe.

THE END
THE BEGINNING

EPILOGUE

As I embraced God's latest call on my life; I was babysitting my grandchildren, Destiny and Justin, on December 27, 2004, when my granddaughter, Destiny, who was four and a half years old, saw my brothers', Dicky and Daryl's pictures, and asked about them. So I told her where they were and what had happened to them. A few days later she said, "Nana, we are all going to die someday. When I get to heaven where Jesus is – I'm going to talk to your bubbies."

"I am too, Sissy."

On February 25, 2005, two months before my grandson, Justin's fourth birthday, he had been playing when he came into the living room and climbed on my lap. A few minutes later he said, staring into the distance, "Nana, I been missing God – now Him dead on the cross!"

"No Bub – Jesus is alive!"

ORDER FORM

To order additional copies of this book, please fill out the form below and mail the form to:

The Alabaster Box
P. O. Box 819
Oologah, OK 74053-0819

....

Please send _____ copies of *"GOD'S GIFT"* to:

Name: _____   _____
                     (Please print name legibly)

Address: _____

City: _____ State: ____ Zip: _____

Phone Number: (_____)_____

I am enclosing $_____ ($10.00 for each book ordered, plus $3.00 to cover shipping and handling. Please make checks payable to The Alabaster Box.)

[Deliveries outside the United States and Canada may require additional postage.]

TO ORDER

THE YEARS OF TEARS and HIS GLORY

Write to:

Helen J. Snider
P. O. Box 451559
Grove, OK 74345-1559

Send $10 per book
$2 shipping and handling
And 8% tax if delivered in Oklahoma

NOTE: ALL REVENUE RECEIVED FROM THE
SALE OF THIS BOOK WILL BE DONATED
TO THE MINISTRIES OF GOD.

ORDER FORM

To order additional copies of this book, please fill out the form below and mail the form to:

The Alabaster Box
P. O. Box 819
Oologah, OK 74053-0819

....

Please send _____ copies of *"GOD'S GIFT"* to:

Name: _____
(Please print name legibly)

Address: _____

City: _____ State: _____ Zip: _____

Phone Number: (_____)_____

I am enclosing $_____ ($10.00 for each book ordered, plus $3.00 to cover shipping and handling. Please make checks payable to The Alabaster Box.)

[Deliveries outside the United States and Canada may require additional postage.]

TO ORDER

THE YEARS OF TEARS and HIS GLORY

Write to:

Helen J. Snider
P. O. Box 451559
Grove, OK 74345-1559

Send $10 per book
$2 shipping and handling
And 8% tax if delivered in Oklahoma

NOTE: ALL REVENUE RECEIVED FROM THE
SALE OF THIS BOOK WILL BE DONATED
TO THE MINISTRIES OF GOD.

ORDER FORM

To order additional copies of this book, please fill out the form below and mail the form to:

The Alabaster Box
P. O. Box 819
Oologah, OK 74053-0819

....

Please send _____ copies of *"GOD'S GIFT"* to:

Name: _____
(Please print name legibly)

Address: _____

City: _____ State: _____ Zip: _____

Phone Number: (_____)_____

I am enclosing $_____ ($10.00 for each book ordered, plus $3.00 to cover shipping and handling. Please make checks payable to The Alabaster Box.)

[Deliveries outside the United States and Canada may require additional postage.]

TO ORDER

THE YEARS OF TEARS and HIS GLORY

Write to:

Helen J. Snider
P. O. Box 451559
Grove, OK 74345-1559

Send $10 per book
$2 shipping and handling
And 8% tax if delivered in Oklahoma

NOTE: ALL REVENUE RECEIVED FROM THE
SALE OF THIS BOOK WILL BE DONATED
TO THE MINISTRIES OF GOD.